Good Food Naturally

Good Food Naturally

John B. Harrison
Mylora Organic Farms

Illustrations by Douglas Tait

J.J. Douglas Ltd. Vancouver

Printed and bound in Canada for
J.J. Douglas Ltd.
3645 McKechnie Drive, West Vancouver

To my family

and

all who love the land.

Acknowledgements

Many wonderful people have shared in the building of Mylora and therefore helped to make this book possible. I most sincerely thank them.

I am deeply grateful to my wife Marian for her help, encouragement and cooperation which never failed me. Her enthusiasm spread throughout our entire family. In the months prior to publication Jim, Mary, Eileen and Pat became loyal boosters while Leo stayed at the typewriter, David looked after the farm and Cathy, Mike and Steve became a cooperative threesome.

The seeds of thought discussed in this book were sown while reading *Pleasant Valley*. This was a gift from my father and it was he who helped me to harvest the ripened crop of experience while Betty O'Neil's faith and way with words provided a welcome "green thumb" for their presentation.

My gratitude also goes to my loyal and devoted staff, particularly Susi Vere. Among my many good friends in the Departments of Agriculture, Gordon Thorpe and John Webster have not only shared their wisdom with me, but have been kind enough to read and comment on my manuscript.

It has been heartwarming to see our faithful customers year after year. The help which has come from many friends in the agricultural field, business and voluntary organizations and the generous publicity provided by concerned persons in the news media, especially Betty Morales, is most appreciated.

The contagious enthusiasm and thoughtfulness of my publisher and his staff have made the completion of this book a delightful experience.

Contents

The Mylora Philosophy

This book differs widely from the current crop
of publications on organic gardening and farming

because

thirty-three years' experience at   Mylora
has convinced us of the soundness
of a preventive rather than a curative approach

because

we continuously asked ourselves:
Why did the insects attack here and now?
not What should we do about them?

Introduction

In many ways, this book is a celebration of the miracle of the soil with its teeming life and its ability to nourish man. It is a call to examine the role of the soil in building up our natural resources. It offers proof that organic farming is the only real solution to the mounting agricultural pollution which threatens almost all the earth.

Many years as an organic farmer have completely convinced me of the soundness, stability and permanence of organic culture. How I came to be one may help establish my credentials for writing this book.

My early years were spent in Sydney, Australia, with summer holidays in the sheep-raising country of New South Wales on *"Mylora"*, (an Australian aboriginal word meaning "deep pool"), my grandfather's sheep station which probably would be called a ranch in North America. Here my time was spent in riding horses, mustering the sheep for shearing, branding and dipping, along with the chores detested by all small boys of my generation, cutting wood, pumping water and carrying things from one place to another. I remember well the chill of those early mornings, the smell of the dust stirred up by the hooves of the sheep and the excited bark of the sheep dogs as they herded wanderers back to the flock.

After leaving school I decided to become a farmer and so went to work at Mylora. Several months of work there convinced me that I needed formal training so I took a two year course at the Government Agricultural Experiment at Wagga Wagga. Many phases of agriculture were included in this valuable course; cultivation and the growing of grains, fruits, vegetables, and fodder; dairying; care and finishing of pigs, beef cattle, poultry and horses. I then qualified as a *"jackeroo"*, an apprentice farmer who lives at the home of the station owner as a member of the family.

My first job as a jackeroo was on a 3,000 acre sheep station in the Snowy River district in N.S.W. where foot rot and lung worm among the sheep were constant enemies. Then I worked in the outback of the western plains of New South Wales in a totally different milieu. The station, one of the largest in the state, extended over an area of 850,000 acres in the hot, dry country and was fifty miles from the nearest town.

The dryness of those western plains introduced many complicated factors which occupied most of my working life at this sheep station. Thirsting sheep often walked for miles following the scent of water only to find their waterhole dried up; they would huddle together to await death unless rescued and transported to other water supplies. When the rains did come after prolonged dry spells, they were frequently too heavy for even this parched soil to absorb. The water would spread out over the ground creating in the low land shallow watercourses several hundred yards wide, and the sheep, by nature unwilling to walk through even a few inches of water, would again require the search and rescue efforts of all hands and the cook.

Although the rains provided welcome relief from the months of dryness and dust, they too brought problems. The growth of fresh, green grass with its laxative effect after a long period of dry feed caused digestive upsets in the flocks which usually led to an outbreak of diarrhoea. These scours combined with the normal body excreta attracted blowflies which laid their eggs in the soiled wool of the sheep. As the maggots hatched they caused great distress and the soiled wool had to be clipped prematurely to offer relief.

Why relate this background? Because I am often today accused of seeing Mother Nature through an optimistic haze and of having no knowledge of the harsher moods of that capricious lady.

Ready to begin farming my own land, I joined my family in British Columbia where I acquired an eighty-acre piece of land on Lulu Island. The nineteenth-century captain of one of the coastal steamers which plied between Vancouver and San Francisco named the island to honour one of the favoured entertainers of the era, but today it is better known by the less frivolous title of the municipality of Richmond.

Situated about ten miles from Vancouver, Richmond has a mild climate with winter temperatures that seldom plunge to zero and the snowfall is minimal—in fact some winters produce no snow at all. The yearly rainfall at Mylora averages about thirty-five inches and mostly falls during the winter months. Summers, too, are moderate with temperatures that rarely exceed 80 degrees, but, as with the winters, the humidity level is relatively high and can be enervating to those unused to such a climate. The entire lower mainland area has become widely known as a prime living and recreational region and is attracting a rapidly expanding population. The proximity of the mountains which rise directly behind the harbour on the north makes it possible for water skiers and snow skiers to enjoy their respective sports on the same day within ten miles of each other.

The central part of the island had evolved over the centuries into a peat bog, and the harvesting of this peat is an important industry today. Blueberries and cranberries are grown in the areas from which the prime peat has already been removed. From the edges of the bog to the outer part of the island, the soil consists of fine clay which at the fringe of the island is mixed with sand. Mylora, itself, is situated between the fringe area and the peat bog. The entire island is below high tide levels, and municipal pumps provide drainage and give protection against high tides and the occasional flooding by the Fraser River which surrounds the island.

October the 23rd, 1938 was the eventful day when I took possession of my property. The farm had been operating as a dairy farm producing milk for the Vancouver market and I continued this operation while becoming acquainted with local conditions. Besides the routine agricultural chores associated with the dairy business, I had also to grow oats, hay, corn for silage, and a few staple food products such as potatoes. Later my programme included fattening beef cattle as well as producing clover seed, sugar beet seed and turnip seed.

Marriage and family responsibilities made the production of a higher return per acre a pressing necessity, and accordingly I planted my first commercial crop of strawberries in 1947. It was a most satisfactory crop that we harvested in 1948 and led to the establishment of our roadside marketing stand that we still maintain.

At the time we were celebrating the bumper strawberry crop and the success of the new marketing venture, we were unaware that a fungus disease of strawberries called Red Stele was to make its appearance in the fall of 1949 and gradually spread throughout all our fields. In fact not until 1971 did we produce a strawberry crop equal to that first harvest.

1947 was a memorable year for another reason as well. It marked the beginning of my belief in the organic method of growing food. It came about with the reading of Louis Bromfield's *Pleasant Valley* and later *Malabar Farm,* both of which document the author's experiences and growing faith in organic farming techniques. Following this delight-ful introduction I pursued the subject in all the books I could find and there were all too few. The reasoning of the authors backed by their experiences convinced me that here was the only sound and natural basis for an agriculture that could be continued indefinitely with better results following season after season. This was a marked contrast to what I had seen of intensive chemical farming where varieties of food plants would no longer grow satisfactorily and once rich fields were deteriorating.

Such a discovery was exciting and satisfying to me. To be con-vinced of the essential rightness of the theory was one thing, but to put it into practice and gamble the financial well-being of the farm on which my family depended was a serious matter indeed.

Converting my farm to an organic one was not only a long and difficult process, but a lonely one as well. There was simply no one I could turn to directly for organic growing advice. My bright beacons of hope were the successes of individuals scattered far and wide, reported in the few periodicals devoted to organic farming.

Anyone operating outside the generally accepted and established routines soon learns that the luxury of complaining and the salve of sympathy over failures are not usually extended to him by his peers. My neighbours and fellow farmers found little ground for common discussion with me, even though our insect and pest problems were sometimes similar, for their suggestions usually involved the use of a newer chemical or increasing the dosage of an old one, while I still pondered over what soil or drainage adjustments should be made. I was firmly convinced that the key to all such problems lay in the environ-ment and particularly, in a healthy living soil.

Experiments at Mylora were like final examinations at school. If the project was a failure, then another year or season had to elapse before conditions were such that we could try again with whatever changes seemed indicated. Insects and disease destroyed crops com-pletely or partially while we were building up the soil. Our goal was to develop within the soil a harmonious, thriving population of organisms and micro-organisms actively involved in devouring waste organic matter and converting it into the ideal soil to nourish the hungry plant roots. While we were building up the soil, we also had much to learn of the other environmental requirements of each of the different plants we wished to grow. Was it too hot for lettuce? Too cold for tomatoes? Too wet for strawberries? Too dry for peas? Too early for beans? Too late for onions? There were always lots of questions to be answered at Mylora and the years that followed my 1947 decision to adopt organic farming techniques have been and still are a continual learning experience.

Among the pest problems we encountered and have controlled through this educational process were Red Stele in strawberries, aphids in dill weed, green cabbage worms, root maggots, club root and aphids in cole crops, crane flies in grass and rust fly in carrots, and the flea beetles, aphids and scab that took their toll of potatoes in various seasons. Through the years spent puzzling, investigating and experimenting, we suffered our share of failures, but successes occurred often enough to encourage further efforts, and were often dramatic enough to convince us that we were on the right road to finding permanent solutions to our problems. Once we learned, for instance, how to grow dill without attracting an aphid attack or pinpointed the biological error that drew carrot rust flies to our crop and corrected it, the problems were solved.

Most commercial growers, on the other hand, approach the pest problem in a completely different manner. The grower has been conditioned to believe that the only good aphid is a dead aphid, so his solution is to obtain the most effective aphicide available. While he seems to have accomplished his purpose for that season at least, several questions remain unanswered: "How much of the potent spray used remains on the harvested food to be ingested by human beings?" and "If the aphicide destroyed only the weaker strain of aphid, how powerful a chemical will have to be used the following years to control the stronger, resistant members of the species which were not destroyed?" Another problem of the indiscriminate use of pesticides is its interference with the biological balance between the organisms that injure the plants and the insects which control them. This balance is commonly known as the prey-predator relationship. Such an interruption opens the door to new outbreaks of insect pests and disease.

We have had our calamities through the years, such as the dark night in 1955 when an unexpected frost wiped out our entire field of strawberries, and others that have tested endurance almost to the point of capitulation. It would have been so easy to return to the apparent efficacy of the chemical aids which we had used on occasion but we finally convinced ourselves that such things must not, under any circumstances, be put on food.

Today, I enjoy freedom from having to go regularly through my crops looking for pests, new and old. Every farmer and serious gardener knows the heartbreak and the feeling of helplessness when seeing a beautiful crop being destroyed by some new pest.

The organic method has a great deal to offer the home gardener too who is, after all, his own best customer and neither has to pay wages nor seek a market. Today the need to restore the soil in his own garden to its natural unpolluted balance is a challenge to every concerned citizen.

The organic method is appealing too, because it is so easy, so available and so simple. So easy because any gardener having knowledge and appreciation of the interdependency of the soil, plants and animals can grow some food organically; so available because the prime requisite is organic material which is inexhaustible, and in many cases merely requires transportation; so simple because in the organic garden there is no need to be concerned about trace elements, chemical formulations, pH factor, and poison sprays.

But if you wish to grow your food organically you must appreciate and understand sufficient of the natural cycles of life so that you can utilize, at the most opportune time and to the fullest extent, "everything that's going for you". Nature alone may not give us the biggest peach, but she will give the most nourishing one, whenever the soil is in balance, organically.

The late President John Kennedy was so concerned when he read Rachel Carson's *Silent Spring* that he commissioned a group of leading scientists with a wide diversity of background to investigate the quality of the environment. The following is taken from their report.

"For example, recognition that 100% mortality of all pests is not required to prevent economic loss in most crops, allows for naturally occurring, pest-regulating factors such as predators, parasites, pathogens, and climate to exert their effects. Full use should be made of available resistant varieties, natural enemies, planting dates, rotations, judicious applications of fertilizers, sanitation, water management and similar cultural control techniques until the necessary information can be obtained for development of more sophisticated and satisfactory systems of integrated controls."

While the case for organic growing could be more clearly stated it could not come from a better authority.

II Why Organic Growing?

"Ill fares the land, to hast'ning ills a prey,
Where wealth accumulates, and men decay."
Oliver Goldsmith

Oliver Goldsmith wrote these words almost exactly two hundred years ago. They appear in an early stanza of the nostalgic, mournful poem entitled *The Deserted Village.* It is a chastening experience to read his prophetic words today on what may soon become "The Deserted Earth". Before it is too late we must reclaim the land, purify the air and waterways and replace materialism with a genuine reverence for life in all its forms. If we fail, future generations will be denied good physical and mental health, perhaps denied even life itself. Surely there is a social obligation for each of us to agitate, to plan and to work towards halting the poisoning, the befouling by wastes and desecration of the most basic life-giving elements of soil, air and water on this, our planet.

How have we been brought to this desperate condition?

In the letter of dedication to his poem to Sir Joshua Reynolds, Goldsmith reiterates his belief that the price of luxury is the destruction of whole classes of mankind. Can we deny his claim? And Goldsmith's concern was only for the passing of the innocent, healthy peasant class, while our concern must be for the danger to our children of the destruction of the soil.

Only in recent years has the press expressed anxiety over the haphazard and indiscriminate use of inadequately tested chemicals on food crops. The full implication of the cumulative effect of the now-denounced DDT and other chemicals on the living and the yet unborn, both through ingestion and soil saturation, has never been faced by the consumer because it has never been revealed by the scientists. In fact do we question just how much more is known about the long-term effects of DDT today than when it was first marketed? Surely an overhaul of earth housekeeping is desperately needed.

If I write with passion and a sense of urgency, it is because for over thirty years I have worked at improving that most sensitive industry of all — the growing and selling of food fit for human consumption. My standards are high and they differ in several respects from the supermarket and glossy advertising standards of food value. Unfortunately, the general public is unaware of both the manner in which food is grown and the nature of the materials which are used to grow it. What I propose is a return to nature's first and basic principles through the widespread practice of organic growing and the consequent elimination of the use of poisonous pesticides. We may still have time to reverse the degenerative processes already in motion, by revitalizing the soil with organic materials so that we can guarantee a never ending supply of foodstuffs to the public, fully nutritious and at the same time harmless to the present and future generations.

The organic grower produces food for the purpose of nourishing people. Since nature is the prime agriculturist, he copies her ways as closely as possible so that the food will be almost completely natural. During the process of growing food organically all forms of life such as birds, bees and insects are given as much care as man himself. The organic farmer realizes that a threat to any form of life is a threat to human life because man is dependent on all lower forms of life. Many poets, philosophers and theologians through the ages have been convinced that all forms of life together constitute one indivisible entity and that damage to any one part is really damage to this entity.

The micro-organisms in the soil are respected as well for they convert the dead and decaying remains of vegetable and animal life into plant food. These organisms regenerate the soil by means of their life processes and enable the plants to grow more abundantly. The plants in their turn provide food for members of the animal kingdom. The organisms in the soil, the plants and the animals above the soil might be referred to as links in the chain of life. A weakness in any link of the chain undermines the strength of the entire chain. It is this chain of life which concerns the organic grower. And it is the increasing awareness of, and respect for it, as evidenced in the music and poetry of our youth that gives us hope for the future.

Orthodox farming tends to overlook, belittle and generally

denigrate the role of the natural forces of life. The orthodox farmer attempts to impose his will on nature because financial return is paramount. The orthodox farmer's concerns, therefore, are those factors which assist him to achieve a good profit. Since *appearance* in modern merchandising is the one and only criterion of food value, it is of prime importance to the farmer. The second consideration is given to the *quantity* of food which can be produced per acre. It is quite obvious that, since these two considerations are the governing forces of orthodox farming, other factors, even that of nourishing life itself, will be of lesser importance.

Unfortunately, under our present economic system, the profit motive outweighs every other. If the grower cannot make a profit, he cannot continue to produce food. Therefore we are faced with a dilemma. Should we continue to grow food for a profit while the product deteriorates in nutritive value, merely to maintain the status quo of our food growing industry? Or could we perhaps change our economic reasoning and make it possible to grow food for the purpose of nourishing our people properly? It must be realized that such a change would involve a recognition by the general public of the proper relation between food and money, appearance and pollution, quantity and quality.

The orthodox farmer is under few restrictions as to the quantity or type of chemicals which he uses to grow food. In the past growers have been advised by government publications that certain chemicals should not be used on crops which are to be fed to beef cattle or milk cows, yet two of these chemicals, DDT and chlordane, were listed among these recommended for use in growing human food. Fortunately authorities have now imposed tighter restrictions on their use. Scientists still know very little about the changes that nature produces in the soil. They know even less about the long term effects of changes in the soil, and ultimately the environment, which are brought about by the addition of chemicals. Despite this, not only do they permit, but they encourage the widespread use of such possibly dangerous materials. The labels on the packages of such chemicals seldom, if ever, tell the user that some neither wash out of the soil nor break down into more harmless substances quickly; nor that they may remain in the soil indefinitely; nor that each successive application can gradually increase their concentration in the soil; nor that the chemicals used may produce ill effects in areas far removed from that in which they are applied; nor that they may affect subsequent crops; nor that they may even change the character of the soil itself.

The orthodox farmer feels that he must destroy pests which threaten to damage his crop since his yield may be reduced. He frequently adopts a blitzkrieg strategy of total destruction. The deadly chemicals which are used may be effective for only a few seasons before the pests develop an immunity to them, and the resulting ecological imbalance in the entire area can become a major problem.

Tax-supported research and laboratory facilities in our universities, provincial and federal departments of agriculture have become partners with industry in testing the safety and efficacy of these chemicals. Should not those who profit by the sales of such materials pay the costs of testing them as well as bear the responsibility for the ecological disasters too often produced by their use?

THE DISCOVERY OF THE PRINCIPLES OF ORGANIC FARMING

If society had paid more attention and adopted the practice and principles of agriculture laid down by Sir Albert Howard at the beginning of our century, the latter part of this century might have been quite different. As a British agricultural officer stationed in India, he was commissioned by his government to salvage the tea industry. Britain was feeling the economic loss occasioned by decline in the profits from the tea plantations. Sir Albert Howard demonstrated the connection between the health of the soil, the health of the plants growing on that soil, and the health of the animals who consumed the plants. He further demonstrated the principles of natural plant growth, which are known today as the basis of organic growing. Howard documented his findings and presented them to the Royal Geographic Society. Subsequently his methods were adopted in parts of the English-speaking world by various determined individuals even in the face of strong opposition. Sir Albert Howard is indeed the father of organic growing.

Hoof and mouth disease was rampant among the cattle in India at that time, and when Howard's work oxen too were infected, he not only cured them but maintained the resistance of his herd through the application of his organic growing principles to their fodder. Fear of this virulent disease has caused many prime cattle in Canada to be slaughtered in attempts to stop its spread and yet I know of no experiments aimed at controlling it by attending to the organic condition of the soil or other environmental factors. Dr. Hans Muller, speaking in Zurich on January fifteenth, 1966, on the subject of foot. and mouth disease, is reported to have said that not one of the 500 farms that adopted organic methods of cultivation and animal husbandry had been hit by the disease even in villages where the animals were heavily infected.

It is strange that Howard's findings seem either unread or ignored. The Soil Association which he founded in England is attracting many new supporters of its principles, and it has even enjoyed some financial encouragement from the British Government.

Sir Robert McCarrison, who was a British medical officer in India at the same time as Howard, not only corroborated Howard's work but pursued the subject further through experimentation and observation. In his investigations of the relationship between sound agricultural techniques and the health of the people, McCarrison visited many tribes throughout India and he was greatly impressed by the Hunzas, a people living in an almost inaccessible area who had independently evolved an excellent agricultural technique based on their observations of nature's way. Their vibrant health, remarkably pleasant dispositions, and the large number of active, elderly people were a striking contrast to other inhabitants of that vast country or even to those of our own supposedly advanced civilization.

McCarrison's work is one of the few properly documented works written by a scientist relating the health of the soil to the health of the plant, health which is transferred to the consumer and inferentially to man.

Unfortunately his ideas were overshadowed by the exciting medical discoveries of the sulfa drugs at the beginning of World War II and the even more exciting discovery of the antibiotics. Mass production made them readily available to the public. But such products were aimed at treatment while McCarrison's ideas were concerned with prevention. Prevention, it should be remembered, is neither as profitable nor as dramatic as cure so it does not usually arouse public attention even though it certainly is less painful and less expensive.

While North Americans like to think of themselves as the healthiest people in the world, the evidence is piling up to prove that this is far from true. When the United States was recruiting men to fight the Korean War, Selective Service figures revealed that about 50% of the men recruited were unfit for service on either mental or physical grounds. When post-mortem examinations were held on 300 men killed in combat, it was found that 80% of them showed early disease of the heart or arteries although their average age was only 22 years! Conversely, few Koreans showed any evidence of these degenerative diseases. And from World War I to the Korean War, a period of 32 years, there was an increase in rejections from 21.3 to 52%. This deterioration of health appears to parallel the progression of agricultural technology. One report from the American Heart Association states that amongst adults 20 years of age and older, 27,000,000 Americans are living with some form of cardio-vascular illness. While it is fashionable to blame the stress and pace of modern life for the steady rise in heart and other degenerative diseases, is it not far more likely

that a lifetime of poor quality nutrition could be responsible for the
weakened tissue that cannot resist for long such diseases? Both
Howard's and McCarrison's work clearly proved that if a living organism
receives adequate diet and correct living conditions it will thrive, but if
some of the necessary ingredients are lacking, the organism will suffer
and its organs degenerate.

The study of degenerative diseases in plants, animals and men
clearly indicated to McCarrison and Howard that their work was
directed to a common goal, a healthy man.

Surely this is our goal too, and it points to the urgent necessity
of melding the sciences of medicine—curing illness, and agriculture—
growing food, so that both can work harmoniously towards this
common goal.

If the melding of these sciences was important in McCarrison's
and Howard's time it is even more important now. For instance, we
know that fungicides control fungi such as penicillium in strawberries
and raspberries. But what do we know of all the effects of agricultural
fungicides on the patient suffering from an acute disease, who under
doctor's orders is taking antibiotics derived from penicillium? Such
questions need answers.

WHAT IS FOOD QUALITY?

When we try to find what constitutes good, bad or indifferent
food, we are groping in unexplored territory. Modern science has little
knowledge of the *quality* of human food in its ability to nourish.
Scientists can determine whether certain components are lacking or
whether they exceed what would be expected to be the average amount,
but this knowledge is purely relative because the optimum quantity is
still unknown. The biological components of food pose an even more
difficult problem . . . chemical analysis of proteins in two foods can be
apparently similar and yet analysis by chromophotography of the same
foods can show a structural difference. It is hard for consumers to
accept the fact that this gap in our nutritional knowledge exists because
it is obscured by a mass of scientific but wrongly directed investigation.
Nowhere was this so clearly made evident as in the furore that followed
the recent U.S. Food and Drug Administration's blanket condemnation
of the dry cereal industry for foisting off on an unsuspecting public
products with little or no nutritional value. The long lists of vitamins,
minerals, percentages and daily "requirements" listed on the packages
and couched in proper scientific terminology were too impressive to be
disbelieved, yet a closer examination of the wording revealed the
emptiness of the claims. Some seem to have been based on the milk
which the consumer himself added to the product. This manipulation

of nutritional claims is reprehensible because it seeks to make a profit out of concern for health. Until we have more exact information as to our nutritional needs so that meaningful standards of food values can be set, we will continue to be taken in by such advertisements.

THE ECONOMIC PLIGHT OF THE FARMER

The marriage of science and industry has melded admirably with the profit system and seems perfectly acceptable providing that it does not affect the health of the public. Unfortunately this is not so and agricultural practices which disregard the laws of nature threaten man's future.

In Canada the potential for growing food is enormous and we produce far more than we need. Some of this food is sold or given to other countries, it is true, but enormous quantities are stored by the farmer waiting for markets.

The knowledge that such quantities of food exist is a reassuring thought, easily dispelling the spectre of famine from the mind. However such comforting insurance against national hunger is a heavy and unfair financial burden forced on to the individual farmers.

It is now recognized that even a small surplus over the market requirements, particularly of perishable crops, can depress the price for the entire crop. Being dependent on nature, the farmer never knows how great or how small his harvest will be, or how much he will have available for sale the next year. It is here that the economics of food products differs greatly from that of non-food products. The manufacturer can easily control the quantity he produces to suit market fluctuations. Should he miscalculate and be unable to sell all the goods he has produced in his regular market, he usually finds an outlet for such unsold goods at a lower price in a different area. Unlike the farmer's crop, this lower price applies only to the goods he could not sell on his own market and does not affect the price of his entire inventory.

Farm surpluses are normal occurrences, but the unpredictability of forecasting them and the cost of storage for them make the farmer's economic position precarious. Coupled with rising labor and equipment costs and the farmer's determination to keep his farm since it is his sole source of income, surpluses play their part in forcing the farmer to take more and more from the soil with each succeeding crop and, in the end, to destroy the very source of his livelihood . . . the soil of his farm.

Chemicals seemed to be a godsend to the farmer on his treadmill of uncertainty by promising a cheaper means to produce crops. He has had no reason to be suspicious of them since they were offered to him by highly trained scientists and were moreover approved by government agencies. When a new chemical is introduced, the farmer who first uses it has the financial advantage of relatively lower costs and/or increased yield. However, once the chemical is widely used and the lower cost accepted, the price of the entire crop drops. In their eagerness to re-capture costs and sell their perishable produce, farmers compete in price and the customer gains. The farmer is then back on the treadmill with the same financial pressure as before. He may have gained a reprieve in the battle to keep his land, but if the land is not only being depleted but poisoned as well, it is a hollow victory. The customer, the consumer, gains food at lower prices but pays the cost in accepting less nourishing food and perhaps suffering adverse effects caused by chemicals.

Another stopgap development in economic farm problems seems at first glance to offer some relief to the retiring farmer. This is the demand for farm land by speculative investors who have no interest in farming. They compete with one another and pay the farmer an inflated price for his land. This inflated and artificial price is completely dis-proportionate to the amount of farm income the land can produce. A farmer wishing to expand his operations cannot afford to buy such land at the inflated price. He can afford only to rent it. As a tenant farmer, without the security and stability of long term leases, such as are common in England, he does not have the same interest in main-taining the fertility of the soil that he had as an owner. He becomes much more interested in obtaining all the profit he can and that immediately, for he may be unable to rent that piece of land again the next year. The farmer who was a thrifty steward of his land is forced to become an exploiter, and everyone loses in the long run. Economics forces more and more farmers off the land and a greater and still greater proportion of farm land is rented. The fertility of the soil then becomes a national issue deserving of serious consideration. In his book *The Quiet Crisis,* Stewart Udall clarifies very succinctly the value of the land in the following excerpt:

> The Warrior chief, Tecumseh, stated the Indian philosophy
> of nearly all tribes with his reply to the demands of the
> white buyers; "Sell the country? . . . Why not sell the air,
> the clouds, the great sea?"

Have education and commerce given us a superior philosophy?

POLLUTION BY THE ORTHODOX FARMER

Two common farm procedures are the main cause of agricultural pollution. The first of these is caused by materials carried from the soil into adjacent water. Some soluble chemical fertilizers which the plants do not use and the manure from careless livestock operations are carried by the rains and natural drainage into the waterways. In the rivers, they cause the marine vegetation to grow more abundantly, and this proliferating growth of water plants uses up increasing amounts of oxygen. The water eventually becomes too oxygen poor to support its fish life adequately. Some idea of the quantity of manure produced from livestock operations can be gained from a statement of Leslie Hileman, Assistant Agronomist at the University of Arkansas Agricultural Experiment Station, in Arkansas; according to Hileman, there are 1 million tons of poultry manure produced yearly. The ammonium nitrate in that manure is equivalent to about 85,000 tons of commercial ammonium nitrate—which is as much as sold in that state in 1970.

The other cause of pollution is the use of pesticides, some of which naturally find their way into local waterways where they, too, pollute the water and damage and destroy marine life. But their lethal effects extend even into the atmosphere and far beyond the area of original use so that even the penguins in their polar regions contain pesticides in their body tissue. The full impact of such materials on ecology is still unknown. Yet their use is widespread and the demand for them increases every year.

III Food and Health

"The soil must be kept in good health if the animal is to remain in good health. The same is true of man. Soil science is the foundation of protective medicine, the medicine of tomorrow."

André Voisin

Food—whether commercially or organically grown—should be judged by the amount of nourishment it provides; surely this is the only valid yardstick. Yet, as has been pointed out, the measuring of the nutritive value is not only an inexact science but is of very little interest to the growers and sellers of our food.

How do animals—who are totally dependent on nature—consume their food? Most species, except carrion, eat their food fresh . . . so fresh, in fact, that it is often still alive. Predators eat their prey immediately after the kill and most of them devour it in its entirety. Should the prey be too large for one meal, it will be either hidden for future consumption or left for smaller and weaker carnivores to clean up. In their natural habitat you seldom see dead birds or animals. Once a bird or animal passes its prime and weakens in strength, alertness and vigour, it falls victim to the law of survival of the fittest.

Grass-eating animals prefer to graze on live, fresh, growing green grass rather than the dried hay they are so often given.

But man is different. Economically, processed food returns a higher profit and is easier to handle and store. The purpose of processing is to destroy any organisms which can cause the food to spoil while in storage. This destruction extends to the life of the food itself so that it ceases to live and is now dead. So it is dead food that modern man is offered in beautiful, living-coloured packages that cover acres of supermarket shelves. By comparison the counters displaying fresh food occupy a much smaller share of the merchandising space.

The increasing quantity of processed food has not only changed the eating habits of entire nations, but it has moved us farther and farther away from acquiring true nourishment from natural, fresh food. We show little concern for the quality of long-stored food unless it begins to deteriorate. Many processed foods are cheaper than fresh foods since industry has developed machine handling and processing methods which are less costly than the handling and losses involved in the sale of perishable, living food and cheapness is always an important factor in the market place.

This popularity of processed or dead food over live, fresh food, is seen by many housewives as a boon for several reasons. Firstly, such terms as "enriched", "fortified" and "supplemented" imply a nutritional value that will guarantee the family a high standard of health and fitness. That such terms are mainly advertising gimmicks and can even refer to the addition of questionable chemicals to food is glossed over. Secondly, the housewife, with her increasingly busy schedule, shops as infrequently as possible and appreciates the unlimited shelf life of the processed food. What a contrast to the French, Chinese or Italian housewife who may make separate shopping trips for each meal! It is no coincidence that each of these nationalities is famous for its reverence for food, flavour, freshness and presentation. Thirdly, the housewife too has succumbed to the scale of values that puts the dollar at the top. Often the food dollar is the only item in her budget that is elastic so it is here that she economizes.

One of the most expensive items on her diet is meat. In an attempt to reduce its cost livestock are "finished" in feeding lots close to large markets. The high-energy, low-forage content of feed-lot diets produces meat that is firmer and more aesthetically pleasing to the consumer and therefore sells more readily. The nutritional content in meat produced by the feedlot "finishing" is questionable as indicated by Michael Crawford of the Nuffield Institute of Comparative Medicine who, in comparing confined animals on high energy rations with free-grazing cattle, said:

"The high fat carcass has been developed with time, and although we may accept it as normal today, it is suprising to realize that we are now eating more than twice as much fat as protein from the domestic carcass; strictly speaking we now have fat production rather than protein. On the other hand, a bovid free to select its own food has a carcass which is 75% muscle and has adequate energy stores (5%)."

The low roughage content in assembly line feeding is thought to be responsible for intestinal problems in many of the animals subjected to it. In 1967 the U.S. Department of Agriculture Inspectors reported that 9.6% of all feedlot cattle inspected were found to have liver abscesses. The crowding of livestock in feedlots also creates conditions in which diseases spread rapidly.

So ever-increasing amounts of antibiotics are being introduced into livestock. Consequently, some medical men suggest that this ingestion of antibiotics by the human consumer of meat, milk and eggs may well build up immunities that will eventually render antibiotics ineffective as a medicine.

Can we possibly have a vigorous, healthy nation nourished with increasing amounts of dead food; with food which is deficient because it has had some of its integral parts removed; with food which is treated with chemical adulterants and is no longer pure? An investigation of this "battered food" syndrome is long overdue and hopefully would resolve the question as to why, if our food is getting better and better, does it need this bombardment with chemicals . . . . and what are the long-term effects of these additions and deletions?

The story of white flour is a classic but bears repetition in this context. The removal of the outer skin and the wheat germ from flour to improve its appearance and protect it from weevils during long periods of storage, renders it relatively ageless but nutritionally lifeless. The wheat germ is a vital factor in the grain, for it contains vitamin E which has been found to be a significant factor in the prevention of heart disease. White flour may be aesthetically pleasing in the eyes of man, but the grain weevils know that there is no life-supporting nourishment in it!

It is impossible to document symptoms or diagnose chemical damage to human cells and tissue caused by the flood of food additives, although tests on animals have proved some of them to be carcinogenic.

Scientists tell us that it is possible to destroy an entire species of birds without ever killing one. Some pesticides interfere with the mechanism for controlling the amount of calcium in the egg shell. When there is insufficient calcium the shell will not be strong and therefore will be easily broken during the hatching process. Other chemicals can inhibit the production of fertile eggs. Rachel Carson's *Silent Spring* raised human concern for bird and animal life; are we not concerned with the damage caused to ourselves by loading our food with superficially tested chemicals? If we have an obligation to future generations to shepherd present resources and to hand them down in a healthy, viable state, then we must *know* the long term effects of food adulteration.

The commercial processor is not alone in impoverishing food. The housewife blithely pares away vegetable skins so thickly that the valuable layer of concentrated protection against invading microbes is thrown out as waste. Can we afford to discard this protective layer and call it garbage?

Storing or home processing of organically grown crops is an effective method of avoiding many of the processed dead foods our stores offer us. It makes it possible to continue to enjoy food whose every component is natural even throughout the winter months when fresh food is so costly. Whether frozen or canned, a minimum of preparation and handling is desirable to preserve fresh garden produce.

Food which has not been processed and is subject to natural decay seldom if ever is poisonous—in fact, organisms which cause decay are often used to enhance the texture or flavour of a food. The various types of cheese are obtained by natural decaying methods. But the decay of processed or dead food is caused by different organisms and some can be fatal to man.

Beauty may be in the eye of the beholder, but the test of flavour is by taste and smell. When offered a choice of foods in the store we too frequently base our decision on appearance alone. Contrast this with the grazing habits of animals. Since the beginning of time, grazing animals have chosen which plants to eat within the limits of their grazing range. The fact that these animals have not only survived but evolved and adapted to changes in environment indicates that the food they chose nourished in them the very qualities necessary for this complex adaptation. The choice of plants made by surviving and evolving animals species is based on flavour and aroma rather than the appearance and packaging which have become man's criteria.

The constant movement of grazing cattle is evidence of their unceasing search for the most desirable food plants.

Many of us have had the experience of offering what appears to be an especially lush handful of grass to a grazing animal only to have it rejected with a sniff of disapproval and of seeing the animal move on to what looks to be a scrubby patch of forage and devour it completely. The proffered grass may have been growing around recent animal droppings and had its growth accelerated by the high concentration of nitrogen in the droppings.

We recently conducted an interesting experiment with our Mylora cows . . . given a choice between a pile of supermarket carrots and a pile of Mylora's organically grown carrots, they unanimously clustered at the pile of Mylora carrots even when we complicated the task by placing a box over the organically grown vegetables. A normal, healthy animal will always choose a balanced healthy ration.

Two vegetables may be apparently identical yet one can be significantly richer in minerals and boast a naturally synthesized protein, while the second may have a differently synthesized protein. Chemical analysis is not enough to reveal protein differences, but Dr. Albrecht of the Soils Department of the University of Missouri has demonstrated by means of chromophotography that there are differences in the structure of the protein in apparently similar vegetables.

An excerpt from *New Hope for Incurable Diseases*, by Cheraskin and Ringsdorf Jr., points out the variation of food quality: "We are told by the Food and Nutrition Board of the National Research Council that we should consume about 60 milligrams of Vitamin C each day. We are led to believe that a tumbler of orange juice contains approximately 60 milligrams. What we have not been told is that different oranges, based upon species, picked at different times of the year can vary as much as fourfold in Vitamin C content. Hence, it is very possible to drink a glass of orange juice each day and still not acquire enough Vitamin C. Thus, food species may possibly contribute in a small measure to the inadequacy of the American diet."

Shoppers buying the largest, most expensive fruits available will be often disappointed by the lack of distinctive flavour in what their eyes told them should have been a premium peach, pear, apple or strawberry. The very fact of tastelessness should indicate something. The least it can tell us is that the produce lacks the substances that produce flavour. Science has no name for these substances since they have not yet been isolated and analyzed: they could be vitamins, minerals, or biological products such as amino acids or proteins. Named or not, the fact remains that there is a deficiency and the consumer loses the substances that ought to have been there.

Sir Robert McCarrison experimented in this way: "Two groups of young rats, of the same age, were confined in two large cages of the same size. Everything was the same for each group except food. One group was fed on a good diet, similar to that of a Northern Indian race whose physique and health were good, and of which the composition is given above. The other was fed on a diet in common use by many people in this country: a diet consisting of white bread and margarine, tinned meat, vegetables boiled with soda, cheap tinned jam, tea, sugar and a little milk: a diet which does not contain enough milk, milk products, green leaf vegetables and whole meal bread for proper nutrition. This is what happened. The rats fed on the good diet grew well, there was little disease amongst them and they lived happily together. Those fed on the bad diet did not grow well, many became ill and they lived unhappily together; so much so that by the sixtieth day of the experiment the stronger ones amongst them began to kill and eat the weaker, so that I had to separate them. The diseases from which they suffered were of three chief kinds: diseases of the lungs, diseases of the stomach and intestines, and diseases of the nerves; diseases from which one in every three sick persons, among the insured classes, in England and Wales, suffers."

Sir Robert found furthermore that he could alter the health dispositions of laboratory rats at will, merely by reversing their diets.

In 1939 a group of 600 medical doctors were empanelled at Cheshire in England to investigate the benefits of the National Health Insurance Act. The results of their consideration were published under the title of *Medical Testament.* The document concluded as follows;

"It seems obvious to us that the new knowledge of nutrition compels our profession to return to the Hippocratic view—in so far as it has abandoned it—that a physician is a naturalist (phusikos) and to take cognisance of the other links of the cycle of nature as well as of man, his patient. For only so can he understand his patient. Without pretension to agricultural knowledge we can appreciate the bearing of Sir Albert Howard's discovery of our work . . . . We cannot do more than point the means of health. Their production and supply is not our function. We are called upon to cure sickness. We conceive it to be our duty in the present state of knowledge to point out that much, perhaps most, of this sickness is preventable and would be prevented by the right feeding of our people. We consider this opinion so important that this document is drawn up in an endeavour to express it and make it public."

IV The Soil, Cradle of Life

"Precious soil, I say to myself, by what singular custom of law is it that thou wast made to constitute the riches of the freeholder? What should we American farmers be without the distinct possession of that soil? It feeds, it clothes us; from it we draw a great exuberancy, our best meat, our richest drink; the very honey of our bees comes from this privileged spot."
J. Hector St. John de Crèvecoeur

In the previous chapters the compelling need for change in food production techniques and attitudes was presented not just as a prophecy of doom and gloom, but with the hope of converting "back-to-the-soil" growers to the principles of organic cultivation. To reap the rewards of independence and well-being from the soil as Crèvecoeur did in pre-revolutionary New York state, the twentieth century farmer must arm himself with a basic knowledge of his land and the teeming life that inhabits and enriches the soil.

Unlike Crèvecoeur, who farmed an almost virgin soil, the grower today has to first concentrate on restoring the soil. By examining its composition and studying nature's ways as described in this chapter, the organic grower can adapt his methods to the particular composition of his own land and efficiently overcome whatever problems of pollution, poisoning or past over-cropping it may present.

Geological scientists tell us that the continuous rains which fell as the earth was cooling produced frequent and heavy flooding. By grinding the rocks together as it moved them along, the action of the water produced smaller pieces which were themselves broken down into still finer particles by further grinding action. The movement of the great glaciers and extremes of heat and cold played their part in the breakdown of rocks until the particles reached the size we now recognize as soil. As the particles were reduced in size, they were more easily carried along by the water and deposited in depressions on the surface of the earth. These first small plots of soil contained within them minerals essential to life. Louis Bromfield called such minerals "the volcanic treasure chest of the subsoil" and he brought them to the surface by planting deep-rooted legumes which tap the source of this mineral wealth. The organic grower who can draw upon this source of nourishment for his topsoil and crops judiciously and conscientiously has a never-ending source of enrichment unequalled by any artificial or chemical means.

LIFE IN THE SOIL

Life can be divided into three distinct categories based on the environment in which each type carries out its life cycle. The first of these is the soil organisms such as insects, bacteria, fungi, etc., many of which are microscopic in size and live out their lives in the soil without emerging. Vegetable life which makes up the second category lives partly in the soil and partly out of it. The third form of life living almost entirely above the soil is classified as animal.

Despite disparities of size and life expectations, each of the three forms follows essentially the same cycle. Each is born, hatched or sprouted, matures and reproduces its own kind, and dies. The forms of life which fall into the first two categories mentioned above usually die in the same place as they lived. As the various forms of life die and come in contact with the earth, the organisms on and in the soil act on the dead material and begin the process of decay. The addition of dead and decaying organisms to the soil over countless generations has added more nutrient to the already-present minerals so that each succeeding generation has had not only more, but a greater variety of materials for nourishment.

As the composition of the soil became more complex, so did the life forms that depended upon it. Plants developed special roots which enabled them to forage farther and farther. These foraging roots searched for the tiny crevices in submerged rock surfaces and by entering them were able to glean the minerals stored there during the preceding millenia. Plant waste substances excreted through the roots acted on the antediluvian rock making the minerals in turn available to the plant. In this manner, after the plants die the soil benefits from the physical action of the widespread root system as well as from the decay of organic tissue. The minerals dredged from the subsoil thus become available to more shallow rooted plants in the topsoil, which has an invigorating effect and when they in turn die they add to the humus content of the soil as the decay proceeds. Even the dead roots of the plants far beneath the soil furnish food for younger foraging roots as they seek their own special mineral requirements.

Any follower of nature's way of soil management shudders when he sees soil left bare and exposed to the destructive forces of the elements for even a short period of time. Nature's protective measure may be appreciated when we realize the various ways in which seeds are transported. Some may be stored temporarily in the foliage of trees or among the fur and feathers of animals and birds, even in their intestines. Eventually they fall to the soil surface so that they always will be available when needed to cover the soil with a protecting green blanket if it becomes exposed, by even such cataclysmic disasters as landslides, forest fires, or floods. Man may find satisfaction in his neat arrangements of cultivated, bare soil ready for planting, but nature plants all year round and resents any and all interruptions of her continuity of life cycles.

In nature we always find a wide variety of plants and organisms thriving side by side, an arrangement we call polyculture. Nowhere in nature can we find a monocultural pattern of plants such as cultivated crops where only one species of plant is grown to the exclusion of all others including weeds. A natural mixture of plants growing in the same area can include tall as well as low-growing plants. There will be plants which leaf out early in the spring, plants which retain their foliage late into the fall, and the evergreens which maintain their foliage all winter. These conditions provide dwelling places and protection for many different forms of insect and animal life.

In commercial farming, large fields being prepared for planting remain bare during the entire cultivation process and for about two weeks after planting until the seedlings emerge. During this period many forms of life, both visible and unseen, will have no shelter. Poor growing conditions caused by bad weather or inadequate soil preparation may check the growth of the new plants rendering them more vulnerable to attack by insect pests. Since the usual predators of the pest organisms were denied shelter prior to the emergence of the plant, it cannot be expected that they will be present in sufficient numbers to check the pests and so maintain the balance of nature. They may be found busily controlling the pests in a neighboring field which offered more hospitality at a crucial stage of their development. Before any other possible predators can multiply sufficiently to check the pests, irreversible damage may have been suffered by the crop plants.

Under an organic growing system a variety of plants adjacent to one another can harbour insects which maintain a balance between themselves and their surroundings even including the pests. Providing there is no thoughtless interference, the insect populations will then remain relatively stable.

A further threat to the natural balance is posed by bare soil which invites erosion. Many of us have heard of the dust bowls of the Thirties in North America. Throughout the centuries man has left multiple trails of erosion to mark his passing. It is hard to believe that North Africa once boasted lush green fields that were sacrificed to the voracious needs of the armies of the Roman Empire. The overcropping of this vast area damaged the soil beyond repair and the ensuing erosion can be seen today in the shifting sands of the Sahara Desert. Drifting sand spells the death of the soil. One wind buries tiny, emerging seedlings and the next exposes their delicate roots to the blazing sun. To reclaim the Sahara and restore the soil to a viable food producing medium would take several lifetimes and a measure of world-wide dedication beyond any thus far documented in human history. The struggles of Israel to bring the comparatively tiny Negev desert back into production after centuries of erosion give us a yardstick of the effort and devotion required to make "the desert bloom like the rose". Necessity alone can inspire such efforts.

China, the oldest civilization, shows the greatest soil contrasts within her own boundaries. Some areas are shockingly eroded and practically valueless, while others, which have been farmed continuously for over 4,000 years, are said to be as fertile as ever. Historians credit the philosophies of Buddha, based as they are on a reverence for all forms of life from the lowest to the highest, for the diligent attention and deep respect generations of Chinese have given to the soil. It is worth noting that it is this facet of the Buddhistic philosophy which has appealed so strongly to many of our young people who are looking for an alternative to materialism and the chasing of profit as a motivation for their lives.

SOIL PARTICLES

The size of particles in the soil varies considerably between coarse gravel and fine clay. The clay particles may be so small as to resemble face powder. The actual size depends not only on the composition of the parent rock from which they came, but also on the force and frequency of the natural grinding and weathering factors to which they were subject during their formation.

It has been estimated that if the outside surfaces of each single particle in an ounce of extremely fine soil were somehow peeled off and laid out on a flat surface they would cover an area of about six acres.

When we realize that the source of mineral nutrients for plants is these outside surfaces and that the minerals they contain are made available by the activities within the soil, we have some idea of the relative value of fine and coarse soils. In addition to their basic advantage very small particles necessarily have more interspaces for foraging roots and furthermore these interspaces function as extra capillary tubes through which free moisture from the subsoil naturally travels up to the roots of the growing plants.

MOISTURE IN THE SOIL

When rain falls, water gradually fills the spaces between the particles of soil, forcing out the air which formerly was present. As gravity pulls the water down to lower levels, air returns to fill up the spaces again. However, not all the water is removed by gravity. A fine film of water surrounds each particle and is held there in spite of gravity. This is the important part of the rainwater for it is the portion that the plant can use. We have already seen that the total mineral feeding area of the plant roots is proportionately related to the fineness of the soil particles. The same principle applies to its water-holding capacity. The smaller the particles the greater the total water-holding surface area. In addition to this water supply the organic material in a fertile soil can hold many times its own weight in water. The free water drains away and eventually enters the rivers and finally the ocean. When the free water is unable to drain from the top soil, the passage of air to the roots is blocked and the plant dies of suffocation. It is essential, therefore, that free water be able to drain away quickly.

MULCH

The water that clings tightly to the soil particles is removed in one of two ways. Either it evaporates directly into the warmer, drier air with which it comes in contact at the surface of the soil, or it is absorbed by the roots of plants and passes up the stems into the growing leaves carrying with it the soil nutrients, most of which are incorporated into the plant before the moisture evaporates from the leaf. The rapid evaporation of water directly from the soil itself can be checked by impeding the free movement of dry atmospheric air through the soil. This can be done by breaking the topsoil down to a powdery consistency and spreading it so as to provide a complete cover for the surface of the soil; it then forms what is called a dust mulch. Such a mulch effectively prevents evaporation it is true, but it has the disadvantage of becoming too dry and inhospitable for the plant roots to function properly. Other forms of soil cover, such as straw, are just as effective without this drawback. In fact, they offer advantages beyond the actual retention of moisture for a longer period.

When soil was originally formed, layers of dead and decaying vegetable and animal matter constituted an excellent mat to check evaporation and also eventually added an extra source of nourishment. Musty hay, dead leaves, grass clippings or even the lowest grade of fir or hemlock, sawdust . . . all organic materials . . . can produce a similar effect. Among these, sawdust alone presents a special problem. The organisms which decay the sawdust use soil nitrogen and so impoverish the plants unless their nurture is supplemented. Sawdust is so fine in texture that it is very easy to mix with the topsoil. If this mixing occurs before the sawdust has completely decomposed, the crops planted in it will of course suffer from a lack of nitrogen and turn yellow. Hay and straw however do not present the same problem since they decompose more quickly and are not easily mixed with soil. Some commercial growers use a thin plastic sheeting for ground cover but it adds nothing to the soil.

Materials which are merely placed on the surface of the soil leave the top layer undisturbed. This layer remains moist and the organisms living in it have the advantage of an increased supply of air because of its proximity to the surface. The greater activities of the organisms in this layer of soil produce more of nature's own special food for the hungry plant roots. Under a hay or straw mulch, new roots of plants grow profusely between the soil and the mulch as well as in the soil itself. The soil under the mulch provides an ideal condition for their development and the plant roots thrive on the extra food thus made available.

The minerals present in the rock from which the soil is formed are not readily lost since they are not water soluble, and therefore not immediately available to plants. Nature has however provided a number of ways to release them to the plant world. One of these methods uses the air expelled by the micro-organisms dwelling in the soil. The carbon dioxide contained therein dissolves in the moisture surrounding the soil particles and produces carbonic acid which in spite of being a very weak acid is capable of reacting with minerals which are then used by the foraging roots and sent up through the plant for metabolism. The excreta of soil inhabitants and the waste substances of the roots themselves aid in changing the minerals into solutions which the plants can use.

These natural activities are greatly accelerated during the growing season. The roots developing rapidly in the warm, moist soil greedily seize on the available plant foods before they can be washed away by the rains and they develop burgeoning systems to forage farther afield for the trace minerals that are so important for maximum life use.

SOIL FUMIGATION

Poor farming methods can damage the soil and create conditions where high populations of undesirable organisms and insect pests overwhelm valuable money crops. Some worried farmers, instead of having a thorough evaluation of the soil and a change in their agricultural methods, turn to soil fumigation as a quick method to re-establish their control over the situation. In farm fields soil fumigation is usually accomplished by pulling an implement with cultivator tynes through loosened topsoil. The chemical—at one time tear gas was used—is forced down through tubes in the cultivator tynes to escape into the loosened soil. The fumes of the chemical then dissipate upwards throughout the soil mass, destroying the pest as they do so. Fumigants affect the various forms of life in many different ways. Some organisms are killed, some are damaged or develop mutations, others are not affected at all.

Two major problems follow soil fumigation. Firstly, some predators which naturally controlled the pest—the prime reason for fumigation—can be more sensitive to the fumigating agent than is the pest. When this occurs, any future natural control of the pest by that effective predator will be more unlikely than ever. Secondly, a pest which arrived in the area after the massive fumigation was completed may be unaccompanied by its natural enemy/predator and for the immediate future may reign supreme and uncontrolled.

Fumigation is at best a short lived expedient. Before too long, the farmer becomes faced with the choice of another fumigating procedure or a costly changeover to the growing of an entirely different kind of crop which is not threatened by the pest he is unable to control. But there may not be another crop suitable to his particular locale which could bring him an adequate financial return, and under our present profit-oriented system of food production there is no way he can afford to do the one thing that would benefit everyone in the long run: namely, to grow soil-improving crops that would restore the natural balance in his fields. The fact that usually he cannot finance the time such a procedure requires makes soil fumigation appear even more desirable to him.

Commercial growers place artificial chemical plant food in the root zone area to stimulate plant growth for the sake of increased production. Some soil organisms sensitive to such chemicals will be adversely affected by it. Other organisms will be stimulated to greater activity even when such activity is not necessarily desirable. This stimulation is temporary and artificial and does not satisfy the plant or organism with its natural food requirements. Roots will blunt their thrust through the soil seeking their normal supply of food in order to feast on the convenient but incomplete bonanza and neglect to forage for the traces of minerals so vital to all forms of life, especially man himself. John Davey, science correspondent for the Observer says ". . . the price (of increasing yields by means of chemical fertilizers) is a steady loss of organic nitrogen in the soil, with consequent changes in the soil structure."

SOIL POPULATION

The inhabitants of a really fertile soil are so numerous that one handful of soil can contain as many organisms as there are people on the face of the earth. The weight of the organisms in one acre of highly fertile soil might even be greater that the total weight of all the domestic animals which can be nourished from the plants grown on the surface of that area. The variety of these organisms is astounding. It includes worms, fungi, insects and bacteria, all of which depend on the decaying remains of previous generations of plants and animals for their development. In turn, they convert the refuse in which they live into ideal plant food easily accessible to the roots of the growing plants.

The substances exuded by various organisms in the soil which react with the mineral content of the fine rock particles to make plant food available also serve the soil in another capacity. Some of these gluelike substances enable masses of fine particles of soil to adhere to one another in highly irregular forms. These conglomerations of fine particles are prevented from compacting because they touch at only a comparatively few points owing to the very irregularity of their shapes and apparent haphazard construction. They give the soil its very efficient structure which resembles the texture of breadcrumbs rather than that of a solid mass.

EARTHWORMS AS CULTIVATORS

In the cultivation of the soil by natural processes, various organisms perform special functions. The most active cultivators are the busy earthworms. They travel endlessly through the soil making tunnels the diameter of their bodies as they go. In order to travel, they literally have to eat their way through the soil. Their digestive juices react with the soil particles which they eat and their muscle contractions move the soil particles along the digestive tube grinding one particle against the other and exposing more of their mineral surfaces to the action of the digestive juices. When the earthworms travel from the subsoil to the surface soil they bring some of the subsoil with them. Since it has been through the digestive tract it is already prepared for incorporation into the topsoil when it is deposited on the surface.

It has been calculated that in the rich Valley of the White Nile earthworms bring to the surface 119.79 tons of castings per acre during the six month growing season. However, a moderate earthworm population will bring annually to the surface of each acre of fertile soil, about ten tons of castings, rich in prepared minerals.

The natural question is what are the indications of a satisfactory earthworm population? Evidence of one earthworm per shovelful is considered sufficient to ensure the continuation of this valuable form of cultivation and soil enrichment.

The earthworm tunnels throughout the soil provide free access for air, water and plant roots. The earthworm lines the tunnels with sticky excretions from its body, which help to hold the tunnel walls intact and to reinforce them against collapsing. The excretions appear attractive to the plant roots since the roots travel along the tunnels growing vigorously as they do so.

Larger insects also burrow between the roots and loosen the soil without damaging the roots to further add to this type of cultivation.

Such forms of cultivation cannot be duplicated by man. He merely stirs the surface of the soil in such a way as to tend to dry it and make it less suitable for nourishing the plant roots. Nature, on the other hand, maintains a moist and loose soil surface by means of her natural mulch of vegetable and animal remains which have been deposited throughout the millenia. The crumb-like structure of the soil remains undisturbed and allows free movement of air in the non-compacted soil mass. The mulch lying on the surface prevents the air in the soil from coming in contact with the drier moving atmospheric air which would increase evaporation and so dry the soil.

Before man commenced to till the soil, almost all the organisms died where they had lived. Their dead remains added to the total nutrients of the soil and very little was taken away from or added to the area. The cycle of life and death was complete and the circle closed, to be repeated over and over again. Protective vegetation kept the surface covered. New seedlings germinated and grew up between the remains of the old, dead plants. Neither the rays of the sun nor pelting of the rain could penetrate the covering with enough force to damage the soil. The sun's rays beaming down on the strong, upright plants energized them to send out more and still more green leaves, to bud and fruit and seed profusely and thus continue and complete their cycles of life.

Man interfered with these processes when he began to cultivate the soil and to take from it all he required for his own bodily needs. A comparable quantity of organic material was lost to the soil forever since man deposited the residue of his food wastes elsewhere than in the area which grew the food. As men multiplied in numbers so did this loss of organic matter. These increasing losses in organic material at this stage in time present such a massive backlog to make up that they constitute a real threat to man's future. Great quantities of food are being moved from vast acreages to areas of dense populations. Here the reckless handling of waste residues of this food constantly aggravates the mounting pollution problem of the cities, while the soil in the producing area is starving for the nutriment of such vegetative wastes.

Human excrement has been efficiently utilized to grow food by various societies for centuries. Modern society however considers such procedure esthetically offensive while at the same time it rationalizes—on a cost basis—the dumping of practically raw sewage into rivers and other waters. Downstream neighbours or aquatic sportsmen fall heir to such questionable benefits. Surely common sense and Howard's "Law of Return" dictates that the disposal area for sewage belongs in the fields which grow the crops. The cost of returning such wastes to the farm field today must be calculated against the far higher costs of renewing environmental quality tomorrow. A few cities do process their sewage and sell it to growers, but the majority are far more concerned with the immediate dollar and unthinkingly dispose of it as cheaply as possible via the waterways.

The safest way to prevent the spread of any diseases which could result from the use of human excrement is to destroy the pathogens by careful composting. The proportions must be correct and excrement must undergo the high temperatures generated after the pile is first assembled and then again when it is re-piled; alternatively it can safely be used in its raw state on non-food crops. Details of composting are given on page 107.

THE EFFECT OF THE PLOW

Many species of microbes exist in fertile soil. Some can move as freely as they wish while others must be carried by agents such as water or insects. In this immobile group are those who thrive close to the soil surface with its greater amount of light, its warmer temperatures and the continued presence of air. Others require opposite conditions, e.g., less air, cooler temperatures and intense darkness. Each inhabits the particular area of the soil which provides the optimum condition for its well being. When a plow inverts the soil it damages whole teeming cultures of micro-organic life. Those that are accustomed to dwelling in the cellar find themselves in the penthouse and vice-versa. Organisms thus removed from their normal living conditions show sharply reduced activity and consequently provide less food to maintain the well-being of the plants. Plowing is responsible for destroying vast networks of tunnels through the soil thus grossly interfering with root growth and preventing the expeditious drainage which is so essential after heavy rains.

The advantages of the mouldboard plow are that it is an effective implement for burying the surface trash—undecomposed vegetation. The clean surface soil which results permits the seeding implements to operate freely. As the plow turns the soil over it loosens the particles moving them against one another; its action might be compared to that of bending a book wherein its pages are likewise moved one against the other.

We feel however that the mechanical advantage of the mouldboard plow is far outweighed by its biological disadvantage. It is many years since we have used the plow on Mylora to invert the soil. We now use the rototiller to chop up the surface vegetation and an implement called a subsoiler which breaks up all the soil below the rototilled layer. If there is not too much surface trash we use a cultivator or disc harrows to make the surface soil fine enough for seeding.

Should my readers wish to pursue the subject I refer them to Faulkner's *Plowman's Folly* and Stout's *How to have a Green Thumb Without an Aching Back.*

MATERIALS TO BUILD UP THE SOIL

If your soil is poor because it is too coarse and sandy and will not hold moisture, the addition of fine clay soil will be advantageous, while conversely if the soil is too heavy and stiff it will be easier to work with the addition of some coarse sand. You will need to be careful however about the source of these soil amendments and make sure that they are not of questionable origin, i.e., that they have not been subjected to any form of pollution. Such materials will certainly improve the physical structure of your soil. If, on the other hand, they involve considerable financial outlay, then that same money would give better returns invested in barnyard manure to improve the biological quality, the most important quality of soil. Incidentally, barnyard manure will also improve the soil's physical texture.

Organic material—well decomposed—applied annually to the soil is the best way to increase soil fertility.

THE ROUTE OF THE RAINDROP

The force of the falling raindrops is absorbed by the plant leaves which temporarily bend under the impact and then return unharmed to their normal position. The raindrops then fall more gently to the next leaf below and most of the water runs down the stalk to the soil, trickling through the protective mass of vegetation. It percolates through the miniscule tunnels in the soil engineered by the worms and insects and then seeps to the lower levels of the soil and eventually the deeper drainage canals.

If the soil is fertile and protected by natural vegetation, the drainage water will be clear. Furthermore, it will not become muddy even as it travels through the soil because the sticky insect excretions which maintain the crumblike structure of the soil are sufficiently resistant to the water. It is the soil which is not protected by organic materials, and lacks the drainage tunnels left by burrowing insects and decaying roots, that is damaged by rain. The surface particles are loosened and the soil beneath is compacted. It is the damaged soil whose loosened particles give the water its muddy appearance as they are carried along. When the movement of the water slows down, this vital component of once fertile soil ends up as silt on the bottom of a river or pond. Standing water on the surface of the soil or sluggish movement of water is always damaging and must be eliminated as the silt plugs the natural drainholes.

The organic grower's daily creed is to respect the soil that nourishes him and his family now, and to labour so that he may hand on to those who follow him a soil of everlasting excellence which will never again be exploited by men.

V Plants

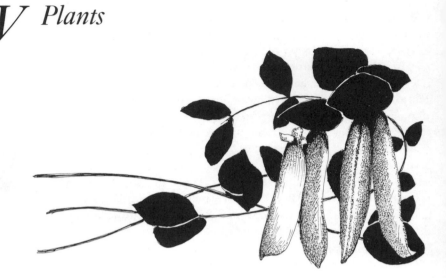

Flower in the crannied wall,
I pluck you out of the crannies,
I hold you here, root and all, in my hand,
Little flower – but if I could understand,
What you are, root and all, and all in all,
I should know what God and man is.

Alfred, Lord Tennyson

THE FUNCTIONS OF PLANTS

Plants provide the vital link between the energy generated by the sun and the energy demands of man and animals. Not only is such energy necessary for physical well-being, reproductive vigour and resistance to disease, but for man, whose continuing creative and intellectual progress is dependent of the quality of his food, the goodness of such plants is crucial.

In addition to providing man with his necessities, plants have the highly specialized function of keeping the quality of the air constant by continuously regenerating the oxygen supply.

When the plant is healthy and vigorous, the leaves are wide open and facing the sun so that the warmth of its rays transpires the leaves' moisture into the atmosphere, leaving in the plant the nutrients which the moisture has carried from the soil. To replace this, more moisture is drawn into the plant roots from the films clinging around the soil particles and from the organic matter in the soil. The fine, hair-like plant roots which have infiltrated the spaces between the soil particles absorb the moisture they require through the outside layer or protective covering of the roots. This passage of nutrient-carrying moisture through the semi-permeable membranes of the roots is the process of osmosis.

When the plants are eaten the carbon contained in the plant provides energy and heat. Some of this carbon is changed into carbon dioxide which is exhaled into the atmosphere from the lungs. Plants use the carbon content of this carbon dioxide to grow more green leaves and at the same time they release the oxygen part so that it can be used once again by animals. This continuous cycling of the carbon and oxygen via the plants and animals maintains a constant amount of oxygen in the atmosphere.

For a plant to function efficiently, all environmental requirements must be met. Only then can it develop fully and provide suitable nourishment for man and beast. We can affect some of these requirements. We have full control over the nutrients available for our plants, but only a limited control over the moisture and the environment. For instance we can grow plants on the north or south side of a building. We may have a choice of a heavy or light soil. We can choose plants which take a long time or a short time to mature. We can sow seeds early in the spring or late in the spring. On the other hand we cannot grow oranges and dates in our temperate climate.

Excessive moisture can be drained from low areas of land, and a moisture deficiency can be rectified by irrigation. Diagnosing moisture deficiency is fairly simple since most plants display definite symptoms when they are short of water. The commonest and most obvious symptom is the wilting of the leaves which is a protective device for the plant. When the leaves wilt and turn down away from the sun they are conserving the moisture which remains in the body of the plant so that the entire plant will not become dehydrated and die. Some plants, including those of the cabbage family, require more moisture than others. If cabbages do not have an adequate supply of moisture, their resistance to aphid attack is lessened, and, unchecked, aphids can eventually destroy the crop.

There are some simple tests to determine the quantity of moisture in clay soil. Take a handful of soil, squeeze it tightly and then release the pressure. If water drips from the soil, the soil is too wet; if it maintains its shape, there is sufficient moisture for the immediate future. If, on the other hand, you can see little sparkles of moisture as you hold it to the light, the soil has all the moisture it can contain. However, if you release the pressure, and the handful of soil loses its shape and crumbles, it is too dry.

When there is a deficiency in the nutrients reaching the plant, there may be indications that all is not well, although pinpointing the exact nature of the deficiency can be difficult. General symptoms of nutrient deficiency are small size, slow growth, unnatural leaf colour and a proliferation of leaves. None of these symptoms can be definitely related to a particular deficiency although the yellowing of the leaves usually indicates a nitrogen deficiency. Magnesium deficiency in corn plants can be recognized by yellowish white stripes in a regular pattern along the length of the leaves. Black spots throughout the fleshy roots of beets indicate boron deficiency; these are more prominent in larger beets, whereas they do not show up so much in the smaller. The symptoms could be caused by other problems such as physical damage to the root system by faulty cultivation or diseases or lack of moisture. There are so many requirements for plants that it is practically impossible to recognize many deficiencies without the aid of soil scientists with their special knowledge and equipment.

A scientific soil analysis can determine some nutrient deficiencies and the scientists will then recommend synthetic plant foods to be applied to the affected crops. However, the success of such a procedure is judged by quantity not quality and is limited by the scant knowledge scientists have about the proportions of soil elements that plants require. Their knowledge of the biological food requirements of plants is so meagre that the subject is not even considered.

About a hundred years ago, a scientist, Liebig, burned some plants and analyzed the chemical constituents of their ashes. From this information he deduced that if a crop contained a certain amount of chemicals then the productivity of the soil could be maintained by replacing the amount of such chemical removed by the plants.

Two hundred years before Liebig's experiment, Jean Van Helmont, a Belgian chemist and physician, planted a five pound willow tree in 200 lbs. of dry earth. For five years he added nothing but rain water to the soil and his tree grew until it weighed 169 lbs. The soil was dried and re-weighed and was found to have lost only 2 ozs. The soil therefore was depleted of very little mineral. A mere 2 ozs. of soil was consumed in growing a 169 lbs. of tree.

Why then are such vast quantities of chemical plant foods used in modern agriculture?

Fortunately, the organic grower does not have to concern himself with such contradictions. He provides adequate nourishment for his unpaid force of workers — the living organisms in the soil — and his deficiency problems are solved.

ROOT EXUDATES

Plant roots growing through the soil absorb the nutrients they need for their development, but they also give off to the soil their waste products or exudates. The organisms, seeds and plants which are in the soil are affected in various ways by exudates. Too many of the same species of plants growing beside one another can create an undesirable or even an intolerable situation as a result of the accumulation of their waste products. Conversely, the exudates of one type of plant can be stimulants for plants of another species and will provide nourishment for their searching roots. Nature makes good use of this factor as can be seen by the different kinds of plants which grow with their roots intertwined. This association of dissimilar species for their mutual advantage is called symbiosis, and is another subject that has received insufficient attention from plant scientists.

When we know how the exudates of specific plants affect one another such information will be invaluable to the organic grower who will then be able to plant his crops to their greatest advantage. At present we do know that marigold roots have a depressing effect on the verticillium wilt fungus, asparagus roots exude a substance which is toxic to nematodes while witch weed germinates only in the presence of stimulants exuded by corn and a few other plants.

In England at the time of the Industrial Revolution, farmers found that if they grew different crops in succeeding seasons in each of their fields, yields were increased and disease was dramatically reduced. This break with the traditional method of planting the same kind of crop in the same field, year after year and even generation after generation, was an important milestone in the history of agriculture and yet the reasons for its successes are still a subject for argument. The reason which was advanced at the time was that the continuous growing of one type of plant in an area used up too much of essential nutrients in the soil, and that these nutrients would thus be in shorter supply with each succeeding growing year. Undoubtedly this is a contributory factor, but a more basic cause would seem to be pollution of the soil by plant exudates. Even the most casual gardener knows the frustration of seeing the weeds which have escaped his hoe flourish with far greater vigour than his carefully tended crop. It is probably that the weeds are being stimulated by the exudates of his crop plants which are themselves being stifled by their own pollutants.

Nature takes care of her soil building, sanitation and pest control by means of polyculture: many plants of different species growing adjacent to one another, and in effect tending one another. Man on the other hand bound by economics is compelled to cling to the convenient monocultural system and is forced to treat each problem separately. The organic grower attempts as far as possible to copy nature and practice polyculture and his reward is a soil which grows vigorous plants to nourish healthy men.

MYCORRHIZAL ASSOCIATION

There is another vital, but almost completely overlooked, way in which plants obtain nourishment from the soil. Known as mycorrhizal association, it involves a special type of root fungi . . the mycorrhiza. This fungus grows on the decaying matter in the soil, and it nourishes the growing plant with the decaying matter. The fine threads of fungus — the mycelia — are attracted by the roots of the plants and grow toward them. One type grows around and attaches itself to the outside of the root, while another grows inside and between the cells of the roots. Both the plant root and the fungus benefit by this invasion. The mycorrhiza appears to obtain more nourishment from the surrounding soil when it is growing in association with the plant root while the plant root actually digests the fungus. Since these fungi are very rich in protein, the mycorrhiza provide a living bridge of protein between the dead and decaying remains of previous generations of plant and animal life and the new and developing plant. The mycorrhizal association is considered by some scientists to be the source of protein which provides the plant with resistance to its natural enemies — insects and disease. In his *Agricultural Testament,* Howard, discussing the mycorrhiza, states, "Its effective presence in the roots of the plant is associated with health; its absence is associated with diminished resistance to disease."

Modern discoveries of the wonder drugs have spotlighted the lowly fungi and forced man to depend on these diligent workers. Perhaps it is logical that the contributions of the fungi should be available to man through his daily food if that food is raised the natural way, the organic way, since these fungi will only flourish and fulfill their bridging role in soil that is well supplied with organic matter. Soils which have been recently sterilized or had heavy applications of chemicals will not provide conditions suitable for fungi development.

SYNTHETIC PLANT FOOD

When plant roots are supplied by artificial plant food placed close around them, they do not have to forage through the soil as widely as normally they would. There is then the distinct possibility that the plant will fail to obtain some of the nutrients present in the soil which are valuable to it but which are not present in the artificial food. Artificial plant foods adversely affect certain organisms in the soil, and thereby interfere with the natural process whereby plants obtain their food. John Davey, science correspondent for the Observer says " . . . . the price (of using chemical fertilizer) is a steady loss of organic nitrogen in the soil with consequent changes in the soil structure." That the addition of some artificial plant foods can be not only dangerous, but lethal, was proved when spinach growers used heavy applications of nitrates to the soil and produced plants with greatly increased foliage. The improved yield of the crop undoubtedly resulted in increased sales for the growers; however, one scientist, Dr. Barry Commoner, has stated that nitrates in spinach have poisoned children in Germany and France, and our own press has reported similar deaths in Eastern Canada.

Potash and phosphoric acid are two other major chemical plant foods. Few people question the source of the contents of those neat bags and boxes as they buy them for their gardens. These substances are mined from natural deposits in the earth that accumulated very slowly over a long period of time and must be regarded as part of our capital heritage. If one continually draws on capital at a greater rate that it is replaced, it eventually becomes depleted.

To nourish a steadily increasing population we must find some source of plant food that will increase as the population increases; otherwise we shall find ourselves in the position of trying to make a decreasing supply of plant food fill an ever-increasing need. Nature's scheme — the use of waste products of previous generations of all forms of life to provide the sustenance for new life — seems most logical and practical in these crucial times, especially now when pollution by waste products is such an omnipresent threat. Paul B. Sears, in *Deserts on the March* has pictured plant nutrition as follows:

"The face of the earth is a graveyard, and so it has always been. To earth each living thing restores when it dies that which has been borrowed to give form and substance to its brief day in the sun. From earth, in due course, each new living being receives back again a loan of that which sustains life. What is lent by earth has been used by countless generations of plants and animals now dead and will be required by countless others in the future . . . No plant or animal, nor any sort of either, can establish permanent right of possession to the materials which compose its physical body."

Such a principle, based on Howard's premise that everything which is taken from the soil must return to the soil, is necessarily all inclusive — human as well as animal and vegetable wastes. In certain sections of China and other countries human waste has been used in the production of food for centuries without any ill effects, whereas in other sections where the waste materials were not correctly treated so that the pathogens were destroyed the communicable diseases have become a health menace.

PLANT REPRODUCTION

Plants are usually divided into the three basic categories of annuals, biennials, and perennials. Annuals are plants which grow from seed and reproduce their own seeds in the same growing season — peas, tomatoes, cucumbers and corn are all annuals. Plants that store up food in a root or head in the first season and then send up seed stalks to produce seed the following year are biennials and include carrots, beets, onions and cabbage. Perennials do not usually produce seeds until the third year, and thereafter will produce seed every year; examples are rhubarb and asparagus. Occasionally a plant from one of these groups will take on the characteristics of another group as in the case of "bolters" in the biennial category. An individual biennial may produce seed in the first year as though it were an annual, but the food portion, i.e., the root, fails to develop and becomes woody and inedible. Such a mutant carrot or beet should be culled even though the seed stalk towers over the other biennials in the field for experience has shown that to plant their seeds in the following season will produce more mutations.

Plant reproduction is accomplished in a number of different ways. The majority of our vegetable plants are annuals and reproduce themselves sexually. The male part of the flower, the pollen, must come in contact with the female part, the pistil, which then grows and develops into seed. Some flowers have male and female parts contained on one bloom. These are called complete flowers, and pollination is accomplished when the male part falls onto the female part. Other plants have their male and female parts segregated in different areas of the same plant. Corn, for example, carries the male flower on the top of erect stems. The developing cob is situated part way up the stem of the corn plant. The pollen must fall on to each of the silken strands which flow out of the cob and then travel up these into the kernels inside the cob in order to complete pollination. If any of the silken threads are missed, the kernels to which they are attached will not be pollinated and therefore will not develop. A walk through a corn patch at the time the pollen is ready to fall impresses even a lifetime growers with the amount of pollen that cascades down from the stem at the slightest touch. A single row of corn planted across the direction of the prevailing wind would be poorly pollinated because the wind is apt to drift the pollen sideways. By the time the pollen reaches down to the level of the corn silks, it will have been blown some distance away from the plant. So corn is never planted in single rows by knowledgeable growers.

Plants which have male and female parts in separate flowers, such as cucumbers and squash, and plants which carry the male flower on one plant and the female on another, usually require the services of insects for pollination. Such plants depend on insects to carry the male pollen to the female pistil, especially if they are not planted close enough so that the wind can help. Plants which put forth an abundance of bloom yet develop few, if any, seeds are victims of incomplete pollination. Fruit trees that display lopsided or unevenly developed fruit, nubby or seedy strawberries, and pea pods containing less than their full complement of peas are all further evidence of incomplete pollination.

Plants that reproduce sexually will vary, just as brothers and sisters have quite different characteristics. Changes in plant characteristics can occur gradually and, as we have seen in the case of "bolters", mutants may show up in any crop. Seed growers must be always on the alert for variants with undesirable qualities to cull them and destroy their seeds and to prevent the propagation of their undesirable characteristics in the following season's crop.

Another type of plant reproduction is the vegetative or asexual method. Dahlias, tulips and daffodils either grow small bulbs around the base of the mother bulb or the mother bulb itself divides into smaller bulbs each one of which is a new, individual plant which can be set out separately. Strawberry plants send out shoots called runners from the mother plant. These runners develop strong roots which thrust downwards into the soil, and, at the same point, send up leaf shoots and a new, independent plant is born. Mint plants grow heavy, lateral roots just under the surface of the soil, and at a short distance from the mother plant; they also send up leaves that will form a new plant. Rhubarb has a large, pulpy root with a number of growing points called crowns. As the plant develops, the size of the root increases and can be divided so that each of the growing points can be set out as a separate plant. Only in rare cases will each new plant reproduced asexually vary and not be identical with the mother plant, whereas sexually reproduced plants will never be exactly the same as each other or the mature plants from whose seed or seeds they have developed. It is, therefore, from sexually reproduced plants that new varieties are developed commercially.

Some shrubs and fruit trees can be reproduced in still another fashion. Layering is a procedure in which a branch long enough to reach the ground is anchored into the soil. Care must be taken to see that the growing tip is not covered. In time the anchored area will develop roots and the growing tip will develop into a normal plant.

Cuttings, which are short pieces of mature wood from the previous season's growth, can be set directly into the soil after all but one or two buds at the top of the cutting have been removed. The buds are the small protrusions along the length of the branch which will make leaves or flowers in the next season. The cutting will develop roots in the soil and the buds form the top growth for the new plant.

Very choice fruit trees and rosebushes are accorded a still different treatment. These varieties may have been bred for unusual colour, size of bloom or multiplicity of fruit, and could have acquired their special qualities at the expense of vigour. Some sturdiness can be restored by joining them to an unrefined vigorous member of the same family with a strong rooting system.

The root of a wild briar is commonly used for strengthening delicate rose plants. Cuttings are first made of the wood of the wild briar and are planted in the spring and allowed to grow naturally through the season into late summer. Buds are then cut from the more fragile species which is to be propagated. In cutting the bud, about half an inch of the bark is left surrounding the bud as it is removed from the wood. If any wood should be cut with the bud, it must be peeled from the inside of the bark. Both bud and bark must be clean so that the bud can lie tightly against the wood just under the bark of the briar cutting. A vertical cut is made into the bark of the cutting about one inch long. At the top of this cut, a second but horizontal cut is made about half an inch long. The corners of the cut bark are lifted up and the new bud is inserted down along the cut in such a manner that the bud point is not covered. All this cut area is bound up snugly, but again care must be taken to see that the top of the bud remains exposed. If this union is successful, the bud will swell a little and in the following spring will put forth its leaves. The wood on the cutting above the new bud can be then removed about an inch above the bud and the new plant is fully ready for complete development.

The necessity for this type of reproduction demonstrates one of the difficulties incurred in breeding plants for specific qualities. The loss of plant vigour during such experimentation has thwarted the efforts of many plant scientists and breeders.

I *Pests and Pesticides*

"*Nearly all the abuses he (man) inflicts on the soil, plants and animals are returned to him in kind, perhaps indirectly, but all the more malignantly because the damage is often far advanced before it can be seen and corrected.*"

Lewis Herber

Through our elementary exploration of the natural method of soil rebuilding and the miracles of plant growth cycles, two roads of departure from contemporary agricultural thinking by the organic farmers are apparent. Firstly, because he follows nature's ways the organic grower takes the long-term view in his planning, planting and protection of his land and resources; consequently, his attitudes differ drastically from those of commercial farmers, and the definitions of such terms as "weed" and "pest" are not blanket denunciations but depend upon the functions that the pests perform. Secondly, he maintains that the common errors in soil management, environmental quality, and growing of plants can be attributed to techniques resulting from the pressing economic necessity of making a profit.

NATURE'S CENSORS

At Mylora, and other organic farms which share our belief, we operate on the principle that the basic purpose of growing food plants is to nourish people and animals adequately and of course to earn for us a livelihood. We feed our families, and sell to the public, produce we know is as nourishing as can be grown and is free from any poisonous materials. We regard so called pests as nature's censors and so resist the blandishments of the chemical companies, because we see no advantage in the total destruction of whole species of insects. We know that normally our vigorously growing healthy plants are not harmed by any insects. We know also that the converse is true, that the sickly plants will attract destructive pests. The destruction of plants by pests is really an enactment of nature's law of survival of the fittest. It is a ruthless law, but the culling of weaklings allows the quality and strength of the species to improve, for only the specimens best suited to the environment live to reproduce.

However the profit oriented grower cannot tolerate the losses occasioned by nature's destruction of unfit plants, so he protects such unfit plants from "pests", for nurturing these second-rate plants may be economically feasible even though it is an unsound agricultural and nutritional practice.

The very word "pest" has an almost completely negative connotation. Yet even in the vast world of the multitudinous pests, it is impossible to divide them into "good guys" and "bad guys" as we shall see in an exploration of insects, bacteria, fungi, viruses and weeds, all of which can destroy food crops when conditions are suitable. We argue that it is agricultural mismanagement that permits crops to be destroyed by pests, and that analysis of massive crop failures usually shows that the pests had everything but an engraved invitation to come in and do their worst.

PESTS ARE PESTS – MAN MADE THEM SO

Recorded history shows that man's agricultural efforts have always been beset by pests. In ancient times serious outbreaks of pests were so rare as to be attributed to the wrath of Gods because of some human offense. In the Biblical recounting, plagues, of locusts and crop failures in Greek and Roman vineyards are usually attributed to breaches of the moral code. It is only in the last century that we have come to recognize that agricultural pest problems are a breach of the natural law and are of man's own making.

"Multiplication of insects and their devastations are largely incited by the degeneracy in our plants and the badness of our culture," wrote Horace Greely, the American journalist, in 1870. Approximately seventy years later, Sir Albert Howard had published his principles of natural plant growing in which he maintained that the plants themselves should be able to resist their natural enemies, insects and disease. Observant farmers recognize that pest problems can be traced usually to areas where the soil conditions are out of balance. Low spots with poor drainage can become breeding grounds for pests; fungi can flourish on plants grown where there are excessive amounts of organic materials, because the materials have not had time to change into a form of food that the plants can use.

VARIOUS PESTS

Insects live above and below the soil surface and are visible in such profusion at some seasons that it might seem that they could take over the earth. Approximately 1,000,000 different species are classified, and some 10,000 are added to the list every year. However, only a very few species of insects attack food crops, and the massive chemical assault that has been launched against these relatively few can be compared only to firing batteries of cannon when a peashooter would suffice.

Fungi

The fine filaments of some fungi inhabiting the soil are almost invisible, others, such as mushrooms, form fleshy, pulpy masses which grow on the earth's surface. A gourmet may balk at admitting that this exquisite delicacy is actually a parasite and a fungus, yet it is both.

An example of a "good guy" is the penicillium fungus which was accidentally found to interfere with the growth of bacteria.

On the other side of the ledger are the fungi that attack our plants and our bodies too. Thus far, the fungus that causes "athlete's foot" has not proved to have one beneficial side effect for man, while the awful destructiveness of the common late blight fungus of potatoes has affected the history of mankind. A prominent historian has said that if it were not for the Potato Famine of 1847 in Ireland, there never would have been a John Fitzgerald Kennedy in the White House in 1960, nor, has said a humorist, would you have been able to find a cop in New York when you needed one.

Bacteria

Among the most primitive of plants is a group called bacteria. Some bacteria in the soil act as pests because they kill the living cells while others act on dead cells and convert them into substances which nourish plants thus completing nature's cycle.

Viruses

Any discussion of pests must include viruses although it is difficult to be definite since scientists in this field are still arguing about whether a virus is a living organism or not. We do know from bitter experience that viruses attack food plants, reduce their yields and cause extensive losses. The virus is transmitted by insects from plant to plant and crop to crop, when they feed from a virus-infected plant and then move to healthy plants. The control of insects has been used by commercial farmers in an attempt to stop the spread of viruses. If the plant is infected with virus it may show symptoms of stunted growth, mottling, and yellowing or crinkling of leaves. A virus causing spotted wilt or curly top can kill tomatoes in a short time but most of the viruses cause degeneration of the plant only.

Weeds

Weeds are pests only when they interfere with the plants we are attempting to grow, and compete with them for food, moisture and light. As an example, when weeds are allowed to grow taller than the cultivated plants, they shade such plants, and this shading even for a short time during the hot growing season renders the plants less able to withstand the sudden shock of full sunlight when the weeds are removed. As a result the growth of the plants is impeded. Several weedings may be necessary while the plants are quite young since most probably there will be additional successive germinations of weed seeds, especially in a wet spring.

When weeds do not compete with crop plants for light, moisture or plant nutrients, their role in soil regeneration is too valuable for us to dismiss them as pests. Weeds serve many useful purposes, and we should concentrate on harnessing them for our benefit rather than trying to eliminate them. Deep-rooted weeds do the same important, soil-building jobs as the plants cultivated by man. They bring minerals from deep in the soil and assist the moisture to rise by capillarity from the subsoil. The grower must consider how much of his time, energy and money should be spent in destroying what could be a useful ally. By covering the earth between plantings, weeds protect the soil from being leached by the rain and dehydrated by the sun and wind. Turned over at the advent of a new growing season, weeds add to the organic content of the soil.

Perennial weeds such as quack grass with their strong root system also build up soil and bind it together. However, because of their special vigour (they will even grow through a potato) they cannot be tolerated in a cultivated area and should be eliminated before a crop is planted.

Sod containing a good proportion of quack grass or other vigorous perennial weeds cannot be controlled satisfactorily by burying. In an old sod most of the roots of quack grass will be growing close to the soil surface under the natural grass mulch. The sod, with a minimum of earth, can be cut off with a sharp shovel and placed in a pile to decay. Alternatively, a 6 inch layer of mulch, such as hay or sawdust, during a single growing season will encourage the majority of roots to grow close to the surface under the mulch where they can be removed by hand.

A crop planted late in the spring provides a longer period of pre-planting cultivation and therefore offers the best chance to clean the area before sowing seeds. Continuous removal of weed shoots as they appear during the growing period will be still necessary to clean the area thoroughly.

WHY INSECTS EAT CERTAIN PLANTS

Research has been done to explain what instincts lead insects to attack defective plants, and the results appear to show that a fine, healthy food plant offers man and animals the best nourishment, for it contains a higher protein-carbohydrate ratio than does an unhealthy plant. Poor plants tested apparently showed a lower protein-carbohydrate ratio.

It is not surprising that insects are drawn to the poorly grown plants with energy rich carbohydrates levels especially when one considers the distance a flea jumps in relation to its size. The energy equivalent in the animal kingdom might be that of the hair-raising sight of a horse jumping over the Empire State Building in a single bound. Man and animals are not only slower moving but their longer life span and great intelligence demand the body-building and repairing properties of protein more urgently than those of carbohydrates. And weather still plays its tricks on the just and the unjust alike as even the most enthusiastic grower will admit. Weather conditions can temporarily favour a speedy multiplication of pests but not necessarily their predators. For example, in our area we know when the soil in the strawberry patch becomes too dry and the temperature too high, the mites multiply seemingly unchecked and damage the crop. This problem is met by having an irrigation system ready to go into action during dry spells.

CHEMICAL PEST CONTROL

This method of control has so many disadvantages that if it were not forced upon people by the demands of the market, it seems unlikely that it would be their method of choice. Let us examine some of its shortcomings.

As has already been said, pesticides, in destroying some pests, allow others to flourish because of the ecological imbalance they create. Target pests may not receive the required dose especially if they are sheltered by leaves or foliage, but they may absorb enough of the chemical to acquire resistance to it. Others may have more natural resistance and will not succumb to the material used. These two particular circumstances can result in the breeding of offspring with greater resistance requiring more and more powerful chemicals to combat them. Of particular interest is the Mrak Commission Report which states:

"When parathion was applied to a cole crop the number of predacious and parasitic species were reduced by 95% whereas the number of plant feeding species were reduced by only 8%. Following this type of disruption, population outbreaks of plant feeders occur. Because the parasitic and predacious species are absent, the plant feeding species increase explosively".

Even if a pesticide were 100% effective in eliminating the pest of the moment, the break in the chain of life would exact a payment in succeeding seasons of growth. The predators who would normally feed on the now destroyed pest either perish for lack of food or move on to other areas. The following year natural predator control will be lacking in direct ratio to the damage sustained by the predators. More artificial control becomes necessary and the mad spiral accelerates with little or no assessment of the complications and damage left in its wake. Even killing mosquitoes has ecological repercussions. In *Man and Nature,* written by George Perkins Marsh and published in 1864 he points out an interesting relationship between the mosquito and the salmon, "By a sort of house-that-Jack-built, the destruction of the mosquito, that feeds the trout that preys on the Mayfly that destroys the eggs that hatch the salmon that pampers the epicure."

In 1945 only 13 pests were found to be resistant to the pesticides then available . . . by 1969 over 220 pests had developed a resistance. Today there are 50,000 commercial products on the market proposing to combat a menace that they have helped to create and that their continued use only aggravates. Surely this attempt to dominate nature has proved to be not only regressive but a losing proposition. As far back as 1952, twenty years ago, the United States Department of Agriculture stated "Never before have so many pests with such a wide range of habits and characteristics increased to injurious levels following the application of any one material as has occurred following the use of DDT in apple spray programs". Our only alternative, which is an alternative for survival, is to co-operate and live harmoniously with nature.

Some scientists estimate that far less than one percent of the pesticides used actually hits the target-pests, while of the remaining ninety-nine percent some adhere to the plant surface to provide protection against pests while the majority is accidentally dis-charged into the atmosphere to cause a colossal amount of unnecessary environmental damage.

Pesticides washed out of the soil and into the waterways will continue to wreak havoc with the marine life they encounter. Such damaging effects stop at neither targets nor boundaries, and their lethal qualities are made even more telling by a factor known as biological magnification. This is a process in which one of the lower forms of life consumes or absorbs some pesticide which is then concentrated in a specific part of its body. When this insect is eaten by its predator the concentration of the pesticide in the predator becomes intensified because of the number of prey consumed. This procedure continues up the biological ladder with each successive and larger predator acquir-ing a more and more concentrated dose of chemical. The ultimate consumer is eventually treated to a massive dose.

Herbicides are chemicals that destroy vegetation. The range of herbicides available today makes it possible to destroy all vegetation in a given area, or to select one which, it is claimed, will destroy most of the weeds in a crop while leaving the food crop unharmed.

These selective herbicides reduce dramatically the cost of weeding crops such as carrots or onions particularly in areas of high rainfall where weed seeds germinate continuously through the growing season. Chemical costs for weeding carrots, for example, might be less than $50.00 per acre, while weeding carrots by hand during a wet spring could cost ten times as much. It is not difficult to see why organically grown, chemical-free crops are more expensive than those treated with herbicides. The cost of herbicides to the farmer is small but the resulting expense to the community is great because, like pesticides, their capacity for destruction extends far beyond the field in which they are used.

The chemical industry has made available to farmers an arsenal of modern pesticides and herbicides which are without a doubt very effective in killing. In order to build sales and subsequent profits, they have employed the talents of specialists in merchandising, marketing and advertising necessary to sustain and expand the industry. At the receiving end of this massive "brain-washing" is the ultimate buyer of the farmer's produce — the housewife. Trained by years of four-colour, glossy magazine illustrations to judge food by its appearance rather than by its nourishing quality, she will refuse to buy food that does not look like the magazine illustrations. So the wholesaler and retailer in turn refuse produce that does not have this "plastic" quality. And the grower is compelled to make certain that there are neither insects nor insect damage on the food he sends to market.

There are materials which are said to be minimally destructive to the environment when applied to plants after pests have already made their appearance. Some organic growers turn their backs on so-called harmless chemicals and use instead such natural sprays as onion, garlic and pepper.

THE RISK

Unfortunately few people realize that instead of containing insect damage which is obvious and can be cut out or washed off, our food contains unknown quantities of invisible, tasteless materials which can destroy our cells at random. Such materials may accumulate in our bodies and injure us years later or affect our genetic cells and produce mutations in our children and our grandchildren such as those following the use of thalidomide. Throughout the world, the effects suspected of being due to thalidomide were limited to comparatively few. Were the earth to have a pesticide disaster millions of children could be victimized. In addition to the tremendous emotional upheaval such a disaster would evoke, even the least materialistic must recognize that the financial price is more than we can afford to pay. Today, it costs taxpayers up to $500,000.00 to maintain one seriously retarded child during a lifetime of full care. Obviously a pesticide disaster must not be allowed to happen, yet we continue putting massive chemical dosages on food plants. In terms of human life modern pesticides are new; therefore we cannot know the effects of ingestion during a complete human life. Nor can we know their full impact on subsequent human generations because there has not yet been one complete generation, let alone the several generations which would be necessary to ensure that no damage occurred.

NATURAL PEST CONTROL

Winter, the slack time in the grower's calendar, is the time for the organic grower to consider his pest control techniques for the coming season based on his successes and failures during the previous season. However serious or trivial a pest problem the grower may have had, its very existence indicates that one or more biological errors have been made. Some questions that would aid in pinpointing the source of the problem are:

Was the soil adequately drained the previous winter?

Was the soil properly prepared and adequately nourished?

Were the seeds or tubers planted, viable and of good quality?

Were the seeds planted at the right time of the year? and some might add, at the right phase of the moon?

Was the area planted to a single species so large that it was monocultural rather than polycultural?

Was a place provided, where beneficial predators could survive during their dormant period?

If such an area was provided, was it close enough to the growing area for the predator to reach its prey?

If any species of plant was pest-infested, was that species of plant suitable to the area?

The convert to organic growing may underestimate the rate at which he can assist nature in the business of soil-building. Organic material, provided it is well rotted, can be added to the soil at any convenient time throughout the year, although it will take usually more than one season to produce a balanced nourishing soil.

Until such a soil is established, the incidence of insect and disease pests in crops is apt to be unpredictable. If one particular crop has attracted more pests than others, it would be wise to abandon growing it until the soil enrichment programme has had a chance to work. If, however, economic necessity dictates a repeat planting of the previous year's troublesome crop, the farmer faces a difficult decision — either he uses natural but admittedly safe materials and salvages what can be only inferior plants or he loses a large percentage of his crop to the same pests or diseases that attacked the year before.

The serious organic grower will choose to assign the difficult-to-grow plants to those fields that present the healthiest soil conditions and will first try with small blocks of them set out among dissimilar plants.

APPLIED BIOLOGICAL PEST CONTROL

Organic farming, or natural biological control, is the maintenance of a hospitable set of conditions in the area so that all forms of life, prey and predator alike, can live in harmony aiding one another; applied biological control on the other hand is the process of introducing predators, such as the lady bug and praying mantis which eat the insects that threaten a crop.

One of the dramatic successes using the predator method of control was the importation from Australia of the Vedalia beetle to wage biological warfare on the cottony-cushion scale that was threatening to destroy citrus crops in California. When the enemy pest was routed, the cost of this safe, effective and natural control method was found to be a mere $5,000.00. Sterilization of males is another method of biological pest control. It has been used successfully among herds of livestock infested with screw worms. Overall, the returns for each dollar spent for biological control are calculated to be about thirty dollars, while a dollar spent on chemical controls will yield a return of only five dollars, and even this diminishes as the immunity of the pest builds up.

The applied biological control has this disadvantage. Should a second pest for which there is no biological control require chemical control, the predators applied to control the first pest could be victimized by the chemical. Applied biological control involves the use of materials and organisms which are not destructive to the environment so that it is far preferable to chemical control. In unusual circumstances such as when a pest is accidentally imported into an area which lacks its natural predator or as in forests, rangelands or non-food producing areas it appears to be an ideal solution. But in commercial agriculture it is preferable to use sound organic practices and to maintain a natural environment which will harbour the predator type insects.

When the aphids attack the cabbages do not apply DDT. If you must, try washing them off with the garden hose or introducing lady bugs, but better still for your next season correct any conditions that weakened the cabbages and made them attractive to the aphids.

II *Planting and Growing*

*"Mixed farming is the secret of success,
no matter how much it complicates the
managerial function."*

Sir George Stapledon

After this exploration of the basic principles of
organic cultivation, I sincerely hope there are thousands of nutrition-
hungry tillers of the soil, with packages of seeds at the ready, prepared
to put it all into operation in a single season. Such enthusiasm is the
stuff required to change the destructive course of modern agriculture,
but before the seed packet is torn open, you should recognize that the
vestiges of poisons used in the past make intelligent planning essential.
And you must recognize that it will take longer than a single season of
sanity to correct soil imbalances and to restore the natural cycles to
your property. The excitement, the triumphs and the amassing of
knowledge of one's own land during a single growing season make each
step toward natural cultivation immensely satisfying.

Rather than deal with the different crops in alphabetical order I
have dealt with them in the same chronological order as we deal with
them at Mylora. This sequence may not exactly suit other areas or
circumstances and will need to be altered accordingly.

Whether you have acreage or a garden plot, planning must be
done well in advance of planting time. One of the first steps that will
pay off handsomely is a complete reconnoitring of the area — learn

from your neighbours what their experiences have been in growing different crops and the diseases and pests that have been encountered through the years. Luckily, farmers and gardeners are far more willing to recount their experiences and secrets than are cooks to disclose their recipes. Undoubtedly you will collect a lot of valuable information. Unless you are lucky enough to be surrounded by organic growing enthusiasts, you will have to evaluate this information in terms of organic principles. But once the "wheat" of this information has been separated from the "chaff", you will find it easier to choose the crops and varieties that are most likely to succeed in your area.

News of the latest super-poison will be of no value, but may make it necessary for you to find protection from its intrusion onto your soil if it is widely used in the community. The good will of your neighbours is most important in requesting that any spraying be done at a time when the wind will not drift the spray on to your garden. If the water from adjoining areas naturally seeps on to yours, a drainage ditch carrying the water directly away should help.

Decisions as to where particular plants should be placed are best made after knowledge of prevailing winds, previous winter conditions and present soil conditions are ascertained.

It is often a temptation for the learning gardener to choose the new, the different or unusual plants so attractively displayed in the seed catalogues, but it is wiser to postpone such experiments until experience enables you to better assess their special requirements. Most of them are only a few generations away from the experimental stage and it may take time to determine if they will thrive under a system of organic-culture.

Within any family of food plants there are enough tried and true varieties to satisfy the tastes of most growers. Planting early and late varieties of the same vegetable ensures a longer harvesting time and a continuing supply throughout more of the growing season. At Mylora we make extensive use of this system of planting in order to keep our customers supplied with the vegetables of their choice throughout the summer and fall seasons.

Given a choice of a gardening site, we would always choose one with a slight, downward slope to the south. The least desirable is one that dips northward. Too steep an incline will permit the soil to dry out too rapidly although it does have the advantage of warming up somewhat earlier in the spring. Before any decision is made to change the contours of the land, it is wise to weigh these factors along with the requirements of the crops planned for it. The organic grower must always take into consideration the fact that radical changes in contours will upset the tiers of the organisms in the soil, and will require special attention until the balance can be restored.

All is not lost even though the garden site faces due north. Heat-loving crops such as corn, beans, tomatoes, squash and cucumbers may have to be bypassed in some areas, but the hardier types such as carrots, beets, parsnips, peas, lettuce, green onions and cabbage can all be expected to thrive in well-balanced soil. Even in the most depressing growing conditions, a devoted gardener can produce miracles by additions of generous quantities of organic materials.

The question of how much of each food crop should be planted is determined by the preferences of the grower and the projected yield of the land available for planting. We offer the following rough guide to yield that you can expect from 1/8th of an acre approximately 20 yards by 30 yards, based on our experience at Mylora; strawberries, raspberries, peas, beans and broccoli will yield approximately 1,000 pounds; cucumbers, cabbages and beets, about 2,000 pounds; potatoes, squash, turnips or onions, about 3,000 pounds — carrots and tomatoes should definitely yield at least 5,000 pounds.

Be careful to plant only the area that is required to provide the amount of food you need. Do not feel constrained to plant the entire area just because it is available. It is far better to leave the unneeded area unplanted and allow it to refurbish the organic content of the soil with natural vegetation. If such areas are kept mowed, they present a neat appearance and weeds will not go to seed. In effect, such fallow fields may be said to be raising their own fertilizer. When such an area is needed for gardening operations in the future, this growth need only be cut up and worked into the top of the soil to complete its restorative cycle.

The choice of plant variety poses a real problem for the organic grower. Many new varieties may be not satisfactory for organic culture. The reason is that the customers who buy the largest amounts of seed are the commercial growers who serve the processing factories or the retail trade, so that seed producers cater largely to their needs. Breeding plants with the characteristics that such customers require can result in the loss of vigour in variety and thus be of little use to the organic farmer whose aim is vigorous plants for maximum nutrition. For instance, processors may demand a variety with the ability to undergo the procedures necessary for their particular form of preservation, while retailers may seek a strain that will maintain an appearance of health for a long period of time after the vegetable is first displayed for sale. Such plants may not do well in organic gardens since their special characteristics may have been gained at the expense of vigour so that they reach their optimum growth only with the aid of chemical fertilizers and pesticides from the moment of planting.

Since many of these varieties have qualities that interest our customers, we have experimented with some of them at Mylora. We have tried very hard to grow small pickling cucumbers but so far have been unsuccessful in producing vigorous plants with a satisfactory yield, yet table or slicing cucumbers thrive in the same field. It appears that plant vigour has been lost in the development of the small pickling varieties we have grown.

So stay with the tried and proven varieties unless you have information from an experienced person that a new variety has proven to be satisfactory over some years. Since seed catalogues and packages do not identify which varieties have been developed for their commercial qualities, it is difficult to find the well established strains. However many of the newer varieties will have initials or numbers in the plant names indicating that they are newcomers and may have been bred for particular commercial qualities.

Planning for every growing season must ensure that the soil is well nourished. The ideal materials for this purpose are properly prepared compost, well-rotted manure and fresh manure: in that order. Compost or well-rotted manure can be applied fairly heavily although the soil surface should still remain visible, fresh manure should be limited to a thin coating. The best time to apply manure is immediately after the frost is out of the ground and the soil is dry enough to work. There it will be worked on by soil organisms and offer a better source of plant nourishment when planting time arrives. If fresh manure is applied to the soil just before planting root crops, the unseasoned manure will tend to make the growth irregular.

SOIL PREPARATION

Probably the most difficult and challenging task facing the gardener is that of preparing to grow a garden on an old sod-grass which has been undisturbed for a number of years. It can tax the body as well as the mind unless a rototiller is available to cut the sod into fine pieces of earth . . . . though even with the use of the revolving blades of this machine it may take two or more treatments to cut the pieces sufficiently finely to make a workable soil. To those who must attack the sod with only a sharp spade, it becomes a temptation to cut out large squares of sod and bury the lot beneath the top soil. However, as has been illustrated already, this is biologically most undesirable. It is better to remove the top layer of sod, pile it up or compost it then return it to the soil when it is decayed. Sod pieces which are cut up and not removed almost certainly will grow again, and if you remove them by pulling them out after you have planted your crop you may also uproot the small seedlings, such as onions or carrots. If the area must be planted before the sod is broken down to a fine workable tilth, it is advisable to plant larger seeded vegetables which will not pull out as easily when the sod is removed.

Sod which has been effectively rototilled must be allowed to dry before it is worked any further. Soil is dry enough when a lump of it breaks and crumbles into pieces under pressure of the foot or hand; if it squeezes into a smaller lump it is too moist. Working a clay soil when it is too wet will produce hard lumps which will be difficult to break up when dry. Sandy soils can be worked earlier in the season, but require greater amounts of organic material to combat their sieve-like texture as well as more irrigation in the warmer weather.

When the topsoil has been loosened up and is moderately dry, the condition of the subsoil should be checked to make sure it is porous and loose enough to allow roots, air and water to penetrate. If it is found to be too compacted the topsoil must be removed, the subsoil loosened to a texture that will guarantee effective functioning throughout the growing period, and the topsoil replaced. Care must be taken to ensure that the respective layers are returned to their original position so that there is as little disruption to the life in the soil as possible. For large acreages, tractor-drawn implements are available which when pulled through the soil hardly disturb the topsoil but thoroughly loosen the subsoil.

Before seeding begins the surface tilth must be correct since it can mean the difference between success and failure. The organic farmer uses the size of the seed to be planted as a rough guide for the size of the soil particles which must be fine enough to cover the seed completely and consequently exclude atmospheric air from coming in contact with the seed. Making the seedbed finer than necessary merely because it is eye-pleasing is not only a waste of effort but unnecessarily destructive to the soil. It must be remembered that once soil structure is destroyed the transference of moisture to the plant is restricted.

Earlier in this chapter, the burying of sod beneath the topsoil was discouraged as being biologically unsound — and so it is. Those who bury such garden trash as clippings, leaves and other dead vegetation commit the same error and impede seriously the natural processes of the soil in making plant food for growth. When undecayed material is buried, it acts as a sponge, preventing the movement of moisture from the subsoil to the surface, and draws the moisture from the topsoil downwards as well. The effect then is to provide a drying agent rather than a feeding system during the growing season. Furthermore, the bacteria living in the airless soil below this spongy mat break down the organic material into an inferior plant food. If, instead, the material is laid down as a mulch over the surface soil, it will be acted upon by the bacteria at the surface which can extract from it the nourishment needed for plant life. This is the natural method of recycling dead vegetation, and it is the method nature has followed in building the soil.

Even after the seed bed is sufficiently fine to begin planting, it will pay to wait a week or two to give weeds a chance to germinate. The tilling done to prepare the soil for seeding will have brought dormant weed seeds into germination, and even though these tiny seedlings are invisible they will be there. One fine raking before seeding will kill those weeds and save a great deal of effort later in the season thus validating the old adage that the time to kill weeds is before you see them. Even a two week delay in planting time will mean little more than a few days delayed harvest, for the plants grow more rapidly with warmer weather.

Do not confuse the organic term, biological balance, with pH level which is the measure of acidity of the soil. Because Mylora is located in an area with high rainfall, it is suspected that our soil is overly acidic, and quite frankly we do not know whether it is or not, since as organic farmers we regard pH readings of the soil as purely academic. We know from experience that well-drained soil that is being nourished with organic material grows healthy, vigorous plants. Briefly, the range of pH readings as related to ordinary vegetable growing conditions is between 4 - 8. A reading of 7 indicates a neutral soil, while any reading above 7 indicates alkalinity, and below 7, acidity. Most vegetable crops grow in acidic soils. Lime is one of the materials suggested to neutralize acidic soils but we have used no lime on our fields at Mylora for over 15 years and still our crops flourish. If we had joined the pH crowd with the litmus paper tests, there is no knowing how much money and time we would have wasted in trying to attain artificially what we have accomplished through the natural re-cycling of organic materials. I vaguely remember an old English saying, "Lime and lime and still more lime makes poor farms and poor farmers poorer and poorer." It is a fact that adding lime can cause deficiencies in boron, iron and manganese even though they are present in the soil.

PLANTING

After this exercise in patience, and with the soil alive and functioning and the particles fined to planting texture, it is at last time to plant the seeds. It works well to lay out the garden with straight lines running parallel to the boundaries. A length of string pulled tightly between two sticks provides an excellent guide for straight lines. The usual technique for planting the first seeds, most of which are small, is to make a shallow furrow with the handle of a hoe or rake to the required depth in the finely-smoothed soil.

Planting small seeds carefully is a tedious job but well worth the effort, since all the surplus seeds will have to be removed at thinning time. It is wise to ensure that they are spaced evenly and economically and there are helpful guidelines at Chart A on page 100 for spacing and depth. Carrots, onions, lettuce, parsnips, or parsley may be planted in a shallow furrow. These seeds require just enough earth to cover them completely, to maintain the moisture and to protect them from the birds which could eat them and any heavy rains that might wash them out of position. Peas and broadbeans should also be planted at the first planting. Chart A indicates the 15th of April for our area. They both require a furrow depth of 1½ inches to 2½ inches.

Peas, beets, carrots, onions, and parsnips will grow to a good size if spaced 1¼ - 2 inches apart, while broadbeans will need 8 - 12 inches between plants. Green onions can be spaced closely - ½ inch apart in a double or triple row since bulb development is less important than a larger green top. Seed varieties incorporating this special characteristic have been developed and are available. It should be kept in mind that spacing of the plants will be determined by the size which the mature plants will attain. Drier growing conditions may require even wider spacing.

At Mylora we have found that the extra labour involved in tying and staking the tall growing peas is not worthwhile so we use only the dwarf varieties of peas. Some growers who prefer tall growing peas place small branches of bush along the rows and allow the peas to climb on these; they then occupy more space than if they were trained to grow up some fishnet or mesh wire but they require less work.

When the time comes to thin out seedlings to leave growing room for them to develop, be sure to follow nature's no-waste policy and use the removed seedlings of beets, lettuce and onion in your spring salads.

The gardener using the conventional monocultural growing methods has to be especially careful not to space plants too closely since their uniform height reduces air circulation and encourages such problems as fungus diseases. The organic method of polyculture with various types of plants growing adjacent to one another has fewer problems with air circulation and plants can be placed closer together thus yielding a greater total quantity of food per acre.

The first spring plantings of the hardy type of vegetables will not be harmed by normal spring frosts but they can be damaged by heavy rains either by washing seeds or seedlings out of position or, in the case of clay soil, by packing the ground and thus preventing the air from circulating normally through the soil. Germinating peas are very sensitive to muddy soil conditions which will not allow any air around the seed and they can quickly succumb to fungus infection and rot. Compacting of topsoil is never healthy or helpful for plant life so hoeing is required after any pounding downpour.

As soon as the first seeds are sown, the seed bed for a second planting should be prepared. Again wait for the next germination of weed seeds before the final raking prior to the second planting, the dates for which are shown in Chart B, page 101. These charts are based on mathematical calculations. However the actual soil temperature is the ultimate governing factor.

A reliable indicator which we use for timing the second planting is that satisfying spring day when the rows of the first planting show the green line of sprouting seedlings. Lettuce usually shows up first and providing that the soil temperature has not dropped below 40 degrees F. since seeding, its appearance can be expected in 8 - 10 days after planting. Onions will follow in 4 or 5 days. Carrots and broadbeans may take as long as three weeks from the seeding date to break through the soil surface.

As the soil will be warmer and drier at the time of the second planting, the seeds must be planted somewhat deeper so they will be completely surrounded with moist earth to be sure of proper germination, Because of higher soil temperatures, germination should occur more rapidly. The soil over this second planting must be pressed down a little more firmly to maintain the moisture close to the surface particularly throughout the sprouting period.

In addition to making a second planting of the first group of seeds you will find it is time to plant beets, potatoes and strawberries. With beets as with lettuce, a high moisture content in the soil is an absolute must for effective germination. If the soil seems overdry, one solution is to mix some of the deeper, moist soil with the surface soil at the time of planting. I suggest this method rather than adding water since only the top couple of inches may be dry while there could be an adequate supply of moisture just below the dry area. Adding water might only chill the soil unnecessarily. This deeper soil unfortunately brings with it not only moisture but new weed seeds as well. The organic grower takes a philosophical and practical view of this mixed . blessing and considers that it is far better to have weeds growing with beets and lettuce than to have neither weeds, beets nor lettuce. Another method of overcoming surface dryness at planting time is to dig a very deep planting furrow right into the moist soil layer, deposit the seeds, and cover them adequately with enough earth, but do not bury the seeds the full depth of the furrow or they may never emerge.

Very small whole potatoes can be used for seed. The more usual method however is to use medium size potatoes cut into chunky pieces with at least two eyes left in each piece. The eye is the small indentation in the surface of the potato from which the sprout will grow. Chunky pieces rather than slivers of potatoes are preferred because the cut area is vulnerable to disease and the smaller the cut area the quicker the surfaces will dry and the better the chance of successful germination. Seed potatoes should be cut several weeks ahead of planting time, dusted thoroughly with hydrated lime, and the pieces stored where there is good air circulation. If the ground dries and warms up early in the season, potatoes can be cut immediately before planting, but it is a gamble since a return of cool, wet weather makes them susceptible to fungus infections and other diseases.

Potato plants take longer than most vegetables to come through the soil surface. Hill up the earth over the tops of the rows of potatoes with earth from between the rows. After a few days, the hilled-up soil can be raked down but not levelled completely. The whole operation can be repeated two or three times and it provides a most effective weed control system. If during these rakings, you remove all the soil from the top of the row you may have difficulty in finding that row again for subsequent hillings. This could result in some of the potatoes being pulled out before they have come through the soil and even if they are put back in immediately, their growth will be retarded. At the time the foliage of the plants is emerging, the soil should be as level as possible. When the potatoes are well up and growing vigorously the rows can then be hilled up again. This time the soil will be around the stems of the growing plants with the soil again sloping away from the plants; the worst weeding days then are over. Subsequent rains could start another crop of weeds germinating, but, with the earth hilled up around the plants, the water runs down the slope without wetting it enough to stimulate weed seed germination. This water may of course germinate weeds between the rows but a fast hoe job will eliminate their claim to the soil nutrients.

The rains could cause a hard, dry crust to form on the soil surface which attracts flea beetles. These insects lay their eggs at the base of the potato plants and when the eggs hatch, the larvae burrow down into the soil and feast on the growing potatoes. Nature, as we have commented earlier, covers the soil and keeps it aerated and of a consistent tilth. Crusted soil is an unnatural condition, therefore it follows that soil not protected by a cover must be hoed to keep it loose and friable.

Once plants have reached the stage that their foliage shades the soil, weeds fade out of the competition for light, moisture and nourishment and are no longer the threat that they were when the plants were at the seedling stage. In fact, weeds now become allies in the march toward a triumphant harvest. This change in attitude toward weeds, from regarding them as unrelenting enemies to possible friendly forces, often proves difficult for new organic growers.

Thus far we have used only vegetables in our illustrations of the practical application of organic principles, but with the increasing concern over the poisonous sprays, questionable food additives and nutritional deficiencies in the food offered in the marketplace, many readers may wish to grow all their food themselves. This is quite possible by organic farming methods and will bring to your tables as wide an array of flavourful and nourishing foods as you could want; and you may even discover that you can enjoy organically grown vegetables such as onions and cabbage whereas when chemically grown they may cause indigestion.

At Mylora we have grown sage, thyme, dill, rosemary, sweet basil and summer savory, from seed which was planted in May, while clumps of chives, pieces of mint, horseradish root, and garlic cloves were planted early in April. Mint has a vigorous root system which rapidly spreads over wide areas so plant it in an isolated area or better still, in a pot. A cylinder sunk around the plant about 18 inches deep will confine the roots. Herbs like a sunny spot but do not need rich soil. If the soil is very rich the growth will be vigorous but lush growth does not have the aromatic quality of slower growing plants. When herbs are planted beside the garden path they grow out over the walk where their leaves will be crushed underfoot. You will then enjoy their fragrance in the garden air.

For centuries, cereals have proved invaluable in sustaining entire nations, and still do. Most of the over-refined sugar-coated forms touted by modern merchandisers are a pale imitation of the robust, flavourful grains in their natural state. Millet grain was the almost exclusive diet of generations of Chinese in large areas of that vast country and the Asian debt to rice as the prime staple of that large continent cannot be denied. Scotsmen would have to rate oats on a par with the clan system in the development of their rugged, self-reliant breed. For food value alone, cereals rate a high priority as subsistence foods. They have the added advantage of being easier to store than root vegetables, with a much longer storage life. Bread rediscovered can be only described as a "happening" when it is baked from your own organically grown wheat, freshly ground in your own kitchen and formed into the aromatic, taste-titillating loaves that should not even have to share the same name as the air-filled, doughy concoctions sold in the stores.

Cereals should be planted out with the second group of seeds in your planning schedule and should present no unique problems if the soil is in good organic balance. Good news for porridge lovers is the variety of oats which has no coarse hull overcoat so that the transition from harvest to breakfast table is uncomplicated by the necessity of hulling.

After the second seeding is completed, the balance of the garden needed for the third seeding as in Chart C on page 101 should be prepared, as before. This third planting will include the heat-loving vegetables—corn, beans, squash, tomatoes, and cucumbers. We begin to plant them at Mylora around the middle of May. We have found it advantageous to plant each kind at about two day intervals.

Beans of the small bush varieties can be planted now and will be ready to harvest before the weather becomes too cold. Pole type beans require a longer growing season than bush varieties and need more labour so we have changed over almost completely to bush beans. The exception is Romano or Italian bean. Because of its tenderness and flavour, we have decided that this pole type is well worth the extra labour involved in growing it. The pod is larger, longer and somewhat flatter than most commercial varieties and so tender that the beans fall apart if they are slightly overcooked. It is this fragility that makes the Romano type unsuitable for the processors so the gardener will find that the seed is difficult to obtain because of small demand. There is a real need for devotees of natural foods to rescue these fragile varieties from extinction by growing seed for discriminating gardeners.

A planting of peas to follow the spring harvesting is practical providing that an early maturing variety is chosen for this summer sowing. These varieties will withstand foggy, fall weather with the attendant mildew problems much better than most of the later maturing types which are also planted at this time of the year.

Included in the third planting are those plants which will mature in the cooler weather such as cabbage, broccoli and cauliflower, which can be directly seeded between the twentieth and twenty-fifth of May, while neither turnips nor cucumbers should be planted until the end of May. Usually cabbage, cauliflower and broccoli are transplanted into the garden, having been started in a nursery bed. Many years' experience has firmly convinced us that the check in growth which these plants receive at the time of transplanting can be sufficient to weaken the plant and consequently it will attract insects, particularly flea beetles, but the aphids and root maggots will also be on the lookout for unthrifty plants of this species.

During this period of adjustment to its new locale the young plants will not be growing at their optimum rate. We therefore plant the seeds of all these varieties directly in the garden in their permanent positions. They are sown more thickly than needed and thinned out subsequently. Be sure to completely remove these thinnings. Dying cabbage plants lying on the soil surface will certainly attract insects.

Radishes are a very short season crop and can be planted almost anytime. However, unless the soil is in very good condition, insects such as flea beetles and root maggots are apt to be a problem. Some gardeners mix a few radishes with various other seeds as they are planted. Since radishes grow quickly they indicate the position of the rows of vegetables and will be harvested before they compete with their companion plants.

Tomatoes are usually grown from plants and it is important that they be purchased from a reputable grower, and that they be delivered in the same box in which they were grown in the greenhouse so the buyer can be sure the roots have been undisturbed and therefore undamaged. The two main types are; (1) the tall vine type which must be staked and tied and knowledgeably pruned at regular intervals, and is the hardier of the two; (2) the short vine bush that requires neither staking nor pruning and is not so hardy as its taller cousin and therefore requires slightly warmer weather before transplanting. These latter varieties are our favourites.

Mylora tomatoes are planted out between the twentieth and the twenty-fourth of May and even on the hottest day we have been completely successful with the following transplanting technique: about four hours before the transplanting is to take place, the lawn sprinklers are turned gently on the tomato plants while in their cartons and continued for the entire period. A very slight depression is made in the soil where they are to be planted. The soil in the carton is cut into sections so that the roots will be cut rather than pulled out. The plant is then eased from the carton with as much earth clinging to the roots as possible and laid horizontally on the soil surface along the direction of the row. Particular care must be taken to ensure the roots of the plants are neither damaged nor exposed to the sun or wind for longer than it takes to remove them from the carton and place on the soil and cover. The tips of the leaves are not bent upwards but allowed to remain horizontal. The root and part of the stem are then covered with fine moist soil which is firmed with a gentle pressure. Be careful not to break the roots by pressing too heavily. Within a few days, the growing tip will have moved to a vertical position and normal growth will continue.

When the plant is placed horizontally against the soil surface, it is kept warmer along its entire length since the surface of the earth absorbs heat during the day and radiates it back at night.

The roots will be stimulated by this heat to reach through the surface and begin to work downward in search of food. Extra roots will grow from the part of the stem that is covered. Instead of suffering traumatic shock from the transplanting process, the plants hardly know that they have been moved, and in a very little time ripe tomatoes will be available.

Leaf lettuce has come to be the variety of choice at Mylora because of the green color it sustains throughout the plant. The outside leaves are as tender as the innermost in contrast to the head lettuce type. This is a personal choice and since both grow well in organiculture, both types can be recommended.

Beets planted in early July will attain an ideal size for fall harvesting if, as with lettuce, they are provided with a good moist soil for efficient germination. Should irrigation be deemed necessary, we have found, at Mylora, it is far better to apply the water *after* the top residues of the previous crops have been removed and *before* the soil is worked. Water falling on an undisturbed soil surface will readily percolate into the body of the soil through root and worm holes and cracks. On the other hand, water falling on finely-worked soil will tend to seal the surface of the loose earth and then run to the lower spots leaving higher areas as moisture-deficient as before, while the lower areas are over-saturated and stay too wet, too long. Evenness of moisture distribution is needed for successful seed germination.

Time is of the essence in summer seeding operations. Irrigated soil will dry out very rapidly, especially while it is being worked. The soil is best left alone during the heat of the day and cultivated in the cool of evening. It is imperative that the seeds be planted as soon as the soil is in a sufficiently fine state of tilth. When seeds are planted in dry weather, the soil must be pressed down firmly enough so that no air passages are left between the seed and the surface through which soil moisture can escape.

Peas, beans and carrots can be planted until the middle of July while broccoli, beets and lettuce can be successfully planted any-time through the end of July. Once August has arrived, the planting season has ended for all practical purposes—only a few vegetables such as chinese cabbage, broccoli and radishes, can be planted after the end of July in our area. Winter cover crops such as fall rye should be planted now or weed seedlings encouraged to develop and spread so that there is as little soil disturbance as possible.

Corn is due now for some attention to ensure a bountiful harvest. Shoots will appear about this time at the base of the corn stems. They will develop into small cobs most of them incompletely pollinated. By removing them the plant matures earlier and grows slightly larger cobs. Also at this time, corn plants need a final hilling with earth which must be piled up carefully around the stems so as not to damage the roots. The purpose of this final hilling is to check the last lot of weeds and at the same time give the roots a better chance to anchor themselves in the soil. This anchoring helps the plants to stand upright even when growing in a soft friable soil and when weighted with heavy, rain-soaked cobs. It is worth the effort since if the stalks collapse before the cobs mature the kernels will not develop fully.

Broccoli and cabbage need watching during hot weather as the all-important soil moisture becomes depleted and insects may then attack. Irrigation will remedy the situation providing there is no club root disease in the area. The spores of this fungus will attack members of the cabbage family when there is a combination of saturated soil and high temperature for the fungus spores to germinate. To prevent such an attack, it is wiser to merely moisten foliage and the top of the soil frequently and wait for a drop in temperature before using full irrigation.

WINTER PREPARATION

Before the garden is left to the vagaries of winter, a survey of troublesome drainage spots is essential. If low spots cannot be filled from a walkway or other area where the loss of soil is inconsequential, be sure to provide a drainage channel to the main ditch. Never allow water to collect and lie stagnant on any part of food producing land.

We made an understandable but costly mistake over twenty years ago in an attempt to solve a drainage problem in one of Mylora's fields which was quite uneven. To overcome the difficulties associated with low spots, we hired a bulldozer to move the earth from the tops of the high spots which was then pushed into the low areas until we had a level field. We were assured by growers who were using the same technique but who had not had their results tested by time, that any damage to the soil would repair itself quickly. However, the massive dislocation of soil and soil organisms turned this field into a continuing problem. It was always the focal point for insect pests, disease and disappointing crop yields, no matter what crop was planted. Only now, after the passage of all those years and the application of countless loads of manure are the soil scars disappearing and today's healthy, luxuriant crops prove that the soil has, at last, come back to full organic life.

Nowadays we remove the topsoil from the outside edges of the field, the areas which serve as roadways and turnabouts for cultivating equipment, and deposit it in the low spots. Thus the field is levelled and natural drainage is provided from the cultivated area since it is now higher, down to the lower roadway and from there to the perimeter ditch. This method has the added advantage that it is permanent. Where the water table is not too high, it is far superior to installing permanent tile or wooden underdrains under the fields. The water that tiles collect has to be pumped out and this requires expensive equipment and services and sometimes the tiles become blocked and cease to function effectively.

Our system, by contrast, requires no maintenance and drains free water away slowly. Without underdrains the water table is higher for a longer period and more moisture is available to maturing plants during the critical growing season.

VIII Harvesting and Storing

"It is everybody's business to realize that what the farmer grows today will be their bodies and their bodies' health and strength, tomorrow."
Sir Cedric Stanton Hicks, M.D.

THE TIME OF PICKING

Pick vegetables from your garden in the cool of the early morning before the heat of the sun evaporates some of their moisture content and at that time the temperature of the plant will be as low as practical. The presence of heat and the lack of moisture both accelerate food deterioration, so early morning harvesting pays a double dividend: it prevents decay and enables the food to maintain that vital quality of freshness for a longer period. But if you soak your vegetables in order to restore their crispness, the surplus moisture on the outside surfaces will cause them to decay in storage.

The first pickings of any plant are the choicest in flavour and are nutritionally superior to subsequent pickings. The variations in flavour between the first and last pickings of certain fruits, particularly strawberries, confirm this. Studies have shown that their vitamin C content drops about fifty per cent in the first two weeks of picking. The sweetness of sugar in the first strawberries is disguised by the tartness of the high ascorbic acid content. As more and more berries are produced leaving less and less ascorbic acid in the plant the sweetness of the flavour then predominates in the later pickings. Those who prefer such smaller later pickings of strawberries, because of their increased sweetness, do not realize that they have lost much vitamin C. Such marked flavour differences suggest marked nutritional differences. Jam makers are cognizant of the exceptional jelling quality of the first berries in contrast with later pickings. The latter often will not jell without the addition of some kind of pectin.

May — The Spring Harvest

The word "harvest" conjures up an autumnal scene complete with bare trees, a dusting of snow on the ground and strutting turkeys. In actual fact, on any organic farm, harvesting and planting are carried out throughout the growing season including springtime. Indeed it is the fall planting of rhubarb and chive clumps that make the earliest spring harvesting possible. The tenderness and flavour of these first crops not only add zest to the palate, but also heighten anticipation of the harvests to come. An early seeding of spinach and radishes with trans-plantings of onions, beets and lettuce will guarantee continuing spring harvests. A word of warning is appropriate here to those who might be carried away by spring enthusiasm untempered by experience: make sure that the soil has dried sufficiently to break up and become loose and soft before planting or your optimistic harvesting schedule will be seriously disrupted.

Spinach is a crop that illustrates the importance of early planting in a well-drained soil. If planted later than March in our soil the heat of summer will produce tough, woody seed stalks rather than the tender leaves of spring-harvested spinach.

Early June — Strawberries

Man is not alone in enjoying the fruits of the harvest. At no time of the year are we more aware of this at Mylora than in early June when the strawberries, choicest of all fruits, begin to ripen. Then we play host to early morning gatherings of birds feasting before the berries are fully ripe. Some of the tactics used in the battle of wits to save fruit have included the placing of pans of fresh water in the fields for the birds hoping to satisfy their thirst and to cut down on their wholesale consumption; other organic growers have suggested that uncultivated fruit which ripens at the same time, such as wild berries, can be planted in close proximity to the market crop and will attract the birds. They seem to prefer their wild, somewhat bitter taste to the comparatively bland flavour of the cultivated varieties preferred by man. Such pref-erence by the birds suggests that some of the nutritive qualities of our sophisticated and newer varieties have been lost.

To enjoy the true, rich flavour of strawberries, you should pick and eat them when they are thoroughly warmed by the sun. They are unlike raspberries whose flavour and piquancy is enhanced by chilling. We will be commenting on flavour a good deal in this and succeeding pages since, like all organic farmers and gardeners, we regard it as a guide to nutritive food value.

Late June — Peas

Spring peas, freshly picked, are a favourite of epicures the world over. Many have vowed that heaven on earth could be attained by following the harvest of new potatoes, green peas and spring lamb around the world. Unfortunately, the increasing labour costs of picking peas by hand may soon cause the disappearance of fresh green peas in their pods from the stores so that only those who grow their own will enjoy them in the future.

The marked difference in flavour between freshly-picked peas from the family garden and canned or frozen peas purchased at the supermarket is accounted for by the differences in every step of production including the selection of the varieties to be planted, growing methods and even the harvesting techniques. Since what happens to peas commercially harvested applies to some other fruits and vegetables as well, let us see how it is done.

Peas destined for commercial canning or freezing are harvested by cutting off the vines at ground level. The entire top part of the plant—stems, leaves, vine and pods—is dumped unceremoniously into a viner which consists of a large drum that is fitted with baffles against the inside wall. As the drum revolves, the vine is carried to the top of the arc. As it drops, it falls on to a series of beaters revolving in the center of the drum. The beaters striking at this mass of vine and pods release more and more peas as the falling pods are struck over and over again by the beaters. Since the walls of the drum are constructed of perforated rubber sheets, the peas fall through to an ascending canvas. Their round shape enables them to roll against the direction of travel down into containers. The pieces of vine and other waste material, being flat, stick to the canvas and are carried over the top of the arc to fall on to the deck of a waiting truck. The action of the beaters also releases much of the plant juices which bathe the peas. This juice seems to implant its own particular flavour to the peas and it is this juice that is responsible for the completely different flavour of commercial grown processed peas from home grown hand picked peas.

End of June — Beet, Lettuce, and Green Onion

After peas come the delicious harvests of beets, lettuce and green onions all of which come to kitchen-readiness at roughly the same time.

Mid-July — Extra Planting

As early harvesting leaves empty spaces in the garden, an immediate planting should be done to continue the process of soil building. If further vegetable planting for later harvesting is not practical in any one year, a seeding of vetch, rye or fast-growing cereal crops will assist in refurbishing the soil as well as covering it quickly. Small weeds may be showing growth at this time and can be encouraged by cutting the tops of the neighbouring taller plants so the sun can get at the weed growth and the soil will be covered even faster than by a planted crop.

At Mylora we sometimes use empty spaces to grow more food for later harvesting. In fact, some crops grow well into the winter months. Broccoli that is seeded early in July usually produces medium to heavy yield. Even after the centre head is harvested, the side shoots continue to grow and are just as palatable as the main head. In our climate such shoots continue to develop until the winter becomes too severe. Lettuce, peas, beans, carrots and beets are other crops which can be seeded in spaces left by the early harvesting.

Leaf lettuce stands up to warm, damp weather much better than head lettuce which tends to rot at the underside of the leaves next to the soil. Our preference for leaf lettuce at our own table is based on its uniform tenderness and the fact that it is more truly a green vegetable. The tough outside leaves of head lettuce may be beautifully green but not so choice to eat, while the heart—supposedly the choice part—is not green enough to qualify as a green vegetable and therefore lacks nutrition according to our criteria.

Summer-planted carrots will not grow to a large size but when grown in a nourishing soil will be tender and can be left in the soil all winter. Such storage is feasible provided that an ample supply of this staple vegetable has been harvested from the main planting and is safely stored against unpredictable weather conditions. If you wish to enjoy carrots fresh from the garden all winter by leaving them in the soil you must be prepared to lose all or some of them by heavy frost.

Raspberries require picking every other day at first, but in extremely hot weather, the accelerated ripening can make daily picking necessary. If the growing season has been a dry one, raspberries respond well to a generous watering at the beginning of the harvest. Early in the spring, only about a dozen of the first husky shoots should have been left to develop while all the others were cut off. By picking time, these shoots will have grown about as high as the fruit bearing canes which made their growth the previous year. The new canes should be tied up so that they will not be damaged when the fruit is picked. After harvesting is completed all the old canes which bore fruit should be cut out at the soil surface level.

Mid July — New Potatoes

About the time the raspberries are ripe and ready for picking some tiny new potatoes can be stolen from the hills without damaging the growing potato plants. Put your hand carefully into the soft soil and feel gently for potatoes. Sneak just one or two small potatoes from each plant, disturbing the roots as little as possible.

New potatoes, as has been noted already, make for memorable dining. A true delicacy they are and highly perishable until the skin is hard and set by which time they scarcely qualify as new potatoes. As long as the skin rubs off easily, new potatoes will not keep very long. Refrigeration is necessary to keep them from becoming soft and even then any area where the skin is broken is vulnerable to invasion by disease organisms which will eventually destroy the potato. The season is short but the flavour is unique.

This points out a well-known but largely ignored fact about the vegetable skins and the area immediately beneath. Here is the first line of defence against invading microbes and here are found the healing and protective qualities which protect the plant and its fruit and which benefit the consumer. To remove the skin with its most valuable disease-resisting layer of flesh and to consign it to the waste bucket is one of modern society's most stupid and wasteful acts.

The harvesting of the second seeding of peas coincides with the raspberry picking. Because the weather will be hotter than that of the first harvest, care should be taken to pick peas in the cool part of the day and if this is not possible they should be cooled rapidly. The heating by the sun, together with the heat which the peas themselves will generate if they are permitted to remain heaped in a container, can affect quality and flavour in a matter of hours.

Beans

The yellow and green beans on the harvesting schedule do not deteriorate as rapidly as the peas and can wait an extra day or two between the pickings during a busy season. They also do not generate so much heat nor does the flavour change as readily as that of the sumptuous pea.

End of July — Cucumbers and Zucchini

Cucumbers and zucchini should be ready for harvest next. There are as many notions concerning the optimum length of a zucchini as there are possible lengths of the squash itself. Personally, I have found little to choose in flavour between a 6 inch and 24 inch zucchini so when you pick them it is a personal choice. If you want young zucchini continuously throughout the summer, you must pick them as soon as they reach about 8 - 10 inches or the plant will stop producing new fruits and direct its energy into the production of seeds. If, on the other hand, a quantity is needed for winter storage, it is better to leave the entire bush (or several bushes) unpicked until the late fall harvest. The small fruits from the remaining bushes should be picked frequently.

Cereal grains such as oats and wheat ripen at about the same time as the first corn and tomatoes are being harvested. In small plantings, the stalks are cut before the ripening process is complete. They are tied in bundles and moved to a sheltered area where the final ripening can be completed. When the seed is completely ripe and dry, it is flailed on a threshing floor where very little is lost. For larger areas the grain is left to ripen thoroughly in the field, to be harvested mechanically. Well-ripened seed heads cannot be moved since many of the seeds would drop off and be lost.

Early August — Corn

Corn—the long-awaited delicacy of late summer—is like springtime peas, a perishable product, and to reap the full flavour and abundant food value should be eaten as soon after being picked as possible. Removing the husks, the protective covering from the corn cobs, hours in advance of using the corn causes it to deteriorate.

Corn requires far more heat than other grains for the seed to ripen. In our area the cobs must be picked when the kernels are well developed and before the weather becomes too wet unlike peas and beans which will ripen on the vine.

Tomatoes

Tomatoes begin to ripen when the corn is ready to harvest. They are best picked when fully ripe. If, however, frost threatens the plants, the tomatoes are picked as soon as they show some colouring and are brought inside to ripen. The only precaution needed to ensure ripening is that the temperature of the storage room must not drop below 50° or they will decay rather than ripen. If tomatoes are left on the vine to ripen watch for weather reports so that you can protect them against frost which comes after mid-September in our area. If frost threatens, you must protect plants. Plastic or other material can be used but if the area is large it could be irrigated. If the temperature then drops to freezing point, ice will form and provide some protection to the plants.

Early September — Winter Onions

Onions should be ready for harvesting early in September. They should be pulled up when the tops have died and have begun to dry up. Leave the roots exposed on the soil surface through several fine days. If the weather is wet and it is necessary for them to remain on the soil for more than three or four days, be sure they are moved at least once after the weather has cleared up, so that all surfaces have a chance to dry. When this is accomplished, the onions are gathered into mesh sacks and placed where there is free air circulation. They must not be piled in a heap but arranged so as to allow free air circulation. To determine the dryness of stored onions, test them by moving them around by hand. If the onions rustle when moved, they are dry enough. A cool temperature is necessary to inhibit sprouting. Onions, unlike other root vegetables, are never hilled up. In fact, if there is earth around their necks they will become thicker and the onions will not cure nor dry satisfactorily, and they will not keep.

Winter Potatoes

Late blight is a nagging worry to every potato farmer no matter how large or small an area he devotes to this staple crop. The middle of August is the time to look for the first symptoms: small dead spots on the leaves. If when the leaf is held up to the light, a moist area is discernible around the dead spot, the probability is that the blight fungus is active and the crop is in jeopardy. If there is any evidence that these symptoms are spreading, speedy action is required. The tops of all the plants in the field must be cut off and allowed to dry up in order to halt any further spread of the disease. The cutting of the tops, if done early enough, will prevent the infection from travelling down the stem into the roots and destroying the potatoes themselves.

Before digging potatoes for winter storage, test some from different areas to be certain that the skins are firm and will not rub off with the pressure of your fingers. A delay of two or three weeks may be necessary after removing the tops before the potatoes have developed a sufficiently firm skin and have reached the optimum state to guarantee good keeping qualities. The drier the soil and the drier the digging weather the longer and better the potatoes will keep in storage.

In areas which are drier than ours, where there is no danger of blight and no problem with excessive soil moisture at digging time, the potato tops can be left to die naturally and their yield will not be curtailed.

Mid September

Dry potatoes, therefore, are the first and most important requisite for good storage. Housed in complete darkness at a temperature of just under 40°, the crop should provide prime eating fare through the winter. Too low a temperature will cause changes that give the potatoes an unusually sweet flavour, while a high temperature will cause the potatoes to dehydrate, soften and lose weight. We usually count on keeping our Mylora crop in prime condition at atmospheric temperature until February. After this time, potatoes left in storage keep better under refrigeration because the lower temperature slows down their sprouting process.

Commercial growers use a chemical that inhibits the natural sprouting process. These materials along with numerous other artificial aids may have many unknown effects on consumers. They are labelled "safe" only because there is no proof that they have caused harm.

Mid October — Carrots and Beets

Carrots and beets for winter storage are harvested while the soil is quite wet so that they will remain firm and succulent for a long time. The Mylora choice of carrot variety—the Nantes—is based on its choice eating quality. Unfortunately it has a tendency to split during harvesting if too full of moisture, unless handled gently. One solution we have tried successfully is to pull the carrots out of the soil and stand them up. stooked like grain, with leaves turned to the sun to extract some of the excess moisture. The commercial trade favours a longer carrot with a tough inner core which bends rather than breaks even when extra moisture is stored in it. Economically sound though this is, it is another example of flavour being considered a secondary factor.

STORAGE

Winter storage for carrots and beets is uncomplicated: the tops are removed and the carrots are piled on top of well drained ground under a four-inch earth covering that protects them from freezing. Should the winter prove severe, a few extra inches of earth can be added for additional protection. The pile can be as long as necessary, but should not be wider than about 30 inches nor higher than about 22 inches. If the piles of carrots are deeper or wider than these dimensions the heat which the stored carrots generate cannot dissipate quickly enough and the temperature within the pile rises. The carrots then begin the second or seed producing phase of their life and nourishment from the carrot will go into the growing roots and the tops which will be discarded. Keeping this in mind, you will realize that the additional earth covering that has been applied during a cold snap must be removed as soon as the danger of freezing is past so that the heat generated by the carrots can be dissipated.

Parsnips and turnips are stored in the same way as carrots. However their flavour will improve if they have been subjected to a touch of frost before being harvested. If the area planted in these particular root vegetables is well drained, they can be left in the ground and dug up as needed. Once the temperature remains constantly below freezing, they can be covered with earth and will keep admirably. Storing these vegetables in boxes of sand in a cool place is also satisfactory.

End of October

The end of October is also the end of harvesting of crops for winter storage at Mylora. As the last of the plants are being pulled, care should be taken to leave behind the weeds still growing among them so that some covering will remain to protect an otherwise bare and vulnerable soil. A dressing of hay, straw, manure or other organic material on the soil surface affords excellent winter protection. It will be found that crops from which only the seed is removed such as cereals, peas and beans leave more residue on the soil surface than root crops so that areas growing seed crops will be better covered with vegetation than areas which grew root crops and consequently will be provided better protection.

Storing food effectively is as important as soil care, planting and harvesting in the farmer's scale of priorities since proper methods and ideal storage environments provide a way of slowing down the life process of food so that it can be consumed in its living state. One of the basic principles of organic farming as laid down by Sir Albert Howard is that living people need living food. Harvested food is still alive and should remain alive if it is to provide the best nourishment.

FREEZING

Freshness is a prime consideration when vegetables are to be canned or frozen. As living organisms they require diligent care and attention, and low temperature and high moisture content must be maintained until they have been preserved or otherwise protected against deterioration.

Food must be frozen rapidly. Smaller packages freeze a lot faster than larger sizes.

To prepare corn for freezing remove the kernels from the cob. This will give extra space in the freezer for additional food. First bring the cobs to the boil rapidly then remove the kernels by cutting with a sharp knife from the stem down; pack them in plastic bags and put in the freezer.

If you intend to freeze strawberries from your own organic garden pick them carefully. If they are dusty and have to be washed be sure to leave the hulls on till after washing. Otherwise the hole left by the core will fill with water which will be difficult to remove. Raspberries can be picked directly into the freezer carton.

SOME THOUGHTS ABOUT COOKING

Hippocrates said that food should be eaten as near as possible to the condition in which nature provided it, so the best way to eat your vegetables is raw, but a steady diet of uncooked vegetables is certainly dull.

Here are a few random hints to help you in the kitchen and at the table, to enjoy all the nutrition and flavour that is in your organically grown food.

Sprouting

Fresh vegetables begin to lose their food value once harvested in spite of the very best treatment, but the seeds of plants such as alfalfa, lentils, mung beans, red clover, rye, soya beans, wheat and most of the other grains or legumes have their vitamin content increased many times after harvesting when they are sprouted.

An easy way to obtain the benefit of sprouting is to place the seeds in a wide mouth fruit jar. Be sure to remove any broken or damaged seeds for they will not sprout and the warmth and moisture will cause them to decay. Several layers of cheesecloth held on with a rubber band can serve as a lid. Rinse the seeds thoroughly twice per day — more often in hot weather — and allow the jar to remain upside-down to drain for a few minutes after rinsing. Since seeds increase in volume about eight times during sprouting allow for this expansion when you first place them in the jar. Sprouting starts better in the warmth and darkness. After about two days expose the sprouts to the light and they will turn green so that you will not only obtain highly nutritional sprouts but a green vegetable as well. Sprouts can be eaten raw or cooked.

Refrigeration

Vegetables which are to be eaten soon should be kept in the refrigerator until they are to be prepared for the table.

The ideal refrigeration temperature for most of the hardy types of vegetables is about 33 degrees, so try to get as close down to this point as possible to give them a longer life. Some vegetables freeze at temperatures just slightly lower than 32 degrees.

Do not wash your vegetables before storing but do so in cold water immediately before preparing for eating. This, too, gives the vegetables an increased life span, for washed vegetables do not keep as long as unwashed. Once the preparation of vegetables has begun and any surfaces have been exposed by cutting they must be protected from contact with the air, so wrap, cover with a liquid, or seal in containers to prevent further oxidation which will diminish their appearance, nutrition and flavour. *The time between preparing vegetables and cooking or preserving them must be kept to a minimum.* Cold air blowing on the vegetables will dehydrate and wilt them; coil type refrigerators which do not depend on air circulation are preferable.

For tender heat-loving vegetables such as beans, cucumbers, squash, pumpkins, tomatoes and others of the frost sensitive type the temperature must be held at about 50 degrees; they will not keep well at low temperatures. Potatoes store well at a temperature of about 40 degrees.

Cooking Chinese Style

The Chinese can give us a lesson in cooking food. Over the centuries they have developed the art of preparing their food with a minimum of nutritional loss.

The main meat and vegetable dish of the day is frequently cooked in a heavy metal vessel with only sufficient oil or moisture added to prevent sticking or burning.

The sauce or thickening is prepared first. The vegetables are assembled and prepared. The meat is cut finely and put into a hot skillet: sometimes they use a wok, a heavy vessel which holds heat well and which is shaped somewhat like a coolie hat without the brim. The meat is seared for a few minutes — pork however is given a longer time — then is removed from the pot and kept warm. Two or three tablespoons of water are added before the vegetables which are then cooked for about 3 - 5 minutes. Since the root vegetables take longer to cook than green vegetables they go into the pot first. When they are well heated and cooked a little on the outside but not soft, the sauce or thickening is poured over them and stirred around for a moment till it too is hot. The meat is then returned to the pot again and put in with the vegetables for the final cooking which is for usually less than a minute. The food is served immediately.

The inside of those vegetables has just been well heated and only a minute amount of nutritional loss has occurred. The entire dish is used, nothing is discarded. If the vegetables were freshly picked then the dinner had the best of nourishment and flavour.

Cooking Western Style

Our method of cooking for long periods in water or fat till the food is soft merely allows the valuable nutrients to escape into the liquid which is then too often discarded. So when cooking vegetables, use only sufficient moisture to prevent their sticking to the pot and burning. A snugly fitting lid will maintain an adequate amount of steam, but steaming in a proper vessel is far superior. Water in which vegetables have been cooked enriches soups and casseroles since it contains many valuable nutrients and so should be saved just as Granny saved it for the stock pot.

Avoid artificial flavourings and colourings for they lack nutrition. Use your ingenuity to enhance flavour and appearance of food. The more palatable a dish is the better it will be digested and the better it is digested the more benefit will be derived from it.

Different coloured vegetables served on a plate not only improve the appearance and help to balance the diet but stimulate the flow of gastric juices, so aiding digestion.

Beans

These should be frenched — sliced obliquely — so that less of the tough protective outside covering and more of the delicate inside flesh is exposed to taste. The beans will then be more flavourful. Romano beans have no strings and can be cooked whole.

Beets

Beets deserve a special mention as a vegetable that can be totally consumed and totally enjoyed. Beet tops — which resemble spinach but are much easier to grow — can be steamed to tenderness in a short time and served with the roots or as a separate vegetable. Cooks should be cautioned not to peel beets before cooking. Indeed, even cutting the tops off too close to the root will bleed the colour from the beet. Once cooked the skin slips off smoothly and the glowing colour is preserved.

Broccoli

Cut the broccoli stems into one half inch pieces right up to the flower, put in a steamer and place the flowers either whole or divided on top of the stalks and steam until tender.

Carrots

Better flavoured carrots result if you slice them lengthwise rather than the usual way of cutting across their length unless they are cut very thinly and fresh carrot juice is a real treat.

Corn

To taste corn at its best, it need not be cooked . . . merely heated enough to melt the butter as you put it on. Those who have tasted fresh picked organically grown corn eschew the practise of adding sugar to the cooking water since the natural sweetness is enough for the most discriminating palate.

Cucumbers

A well chilled cucumber destined for pickling or table use will retain its crispness far better.

Herbs

For winter storage spring seeded herbs must be gathered just when the plants are fully developed but before they start to ripen. When well dried they should be tied in small bunches and hung heads downwards in a dry airy room away from the light. Leaves and seeds should be ground just prior to use, otherwise they lose their piquancy rapidly. Fresh herbs can be stored in airtight containers in the refrigerator. For gourmet cooking, nothing replaces herbs fresh from the garden. The purpose of seasoning is to enhance the flavour not to disguise it. Use herbs sparingly; we all know the effectiveness of a little garlic.

(To the many medicinal values attributed to garlic the Russians have added yet another; they have discovered that when garlic oil is applied to the lips of a wound it kills the most virulent bacteria in ten minutes.)

Peas

We are such devotees of this delicacy at Mylora that sometimes it is only the hard skeleton of the pea pod that finds its way to the compost heap. Empty pods are simmered in a pot until the flesh overlaying the skeleton becomes tender. The skeleton is held between the teeth. The flesh is stripped off and eaten. The flavour resembles that of peas. Even the stock in which they are cooked can be saved to contribute its unique flavour to soups and stews.

Potatoes

When properly cooked, an organically grown steamed potato is a superb dish. It does not need sour cream, chives, bacon, butter, milk, pepper or even salt. Just the potato!! If the potato is large, divide it into egg size pieces and if you do not have a steamer boil it in a saucepan with a snugly fitting lid with just enough water to prevent burning. Cook until the outside of the potato is soft then drain the water; replace the lid, remove from stove and keep the saucepan hot and allow potatoes to finish cooking themselves. Serve immediately since almost all the vitamin C will disappear within an hour.

Salads

Because of their large amounts of enzymes, green vegetable salads should be eaten first to assist in digesting the protein content of the subsequent dishes. Lettuce should be torn rather than cut since it has a more pleasing appearance and it does not wilt so rapidly. Herbs, either fresh or dried, finely chopped and added to a tossed salad are a tasty substitute for an oil dressing, or if you use a dressing, adding herbs enhances it.

Salt

A small amount sprinkled as the food is being served can be just as effective as a larger amount used during cooking.

Soda

Organically grown, freshly harvested, carefully prepared vegetables which are cooked and served quickly retain their superb flavour and they do not require soda to maintain their green colour.

Soup

Mixed vegetables plus your favourite seasoning placed in a blender and ground as finely as you wish will provide a good soup base. Merely add boiling water for almost instant soup.

Squash

Cut in pieces, place sections in a baking dish with a little water to steam, cover the dish, cook until tender.

Tomatoes

Small and sun ripened they can be frozen whole; if necessary wash but dry thoroughly and put in bags. During the long winter months they really add fresh flavour to soups and casseroles.

Zucchini

Slice about one quarter of an inch thick, simmer in tomato juice with a little chopped onion and your favourite herbs. They can also be eaten raw, if they are sliced thinly and served with a little dressing garnished with herbs.

IX *Doing Your Own Thing*

"Good - Better - Best
Never let it rest,
Till your good is better
And your better, best."

This little inspirational verse was moulded into the steel plates at the back of the horsedrawn Furfy watercart and must be emblazoned in the mind of every Australian farmer who ever carried water to thirsty animals. It is good advice to the convert to organic cultivation and I pass it on as a reminder that the quality of the earth as our prime resource must be constantly improved.

The summer of 1971 offered heartening evidence of growing public concern when, as a result of many requests, we set aside part of Mylora for teaching organic growing methods to about 120 enthusiasts. I had given a course earlier during the school year that covered the basic principles of organic farming, and it was mainly the students from this course that participated in our practical programme. Plots of organically-prepared soil, 20 ft. x 25 ft., were measured out for each of the sixty participating couples and the aim was to provide the normal vegetable requirements for a family of four for the summer months from each of the plots. This was accomplished most satisfactorily. Mylora contracted to provide seeds and plants for a dozen easy-to-grow vegetables, along with necessary tools. We also prepared the soil for planting, and I gave weekly instructions on the growing phases as the season progressed.

The learning and working together experience was an enriching one for all of us. Our very diversity — there were professionals, artists, tradesmen, students and housewives — enlivened our discussions and there was just as wide a range of gardening experiences, some having gardened for years using chemical fertilizers and pest control and others having never planted a seed before.

An evaluation of the project at the end of the summer showed that an average of only two hours of work twice per week was required on each of the plots to learn how to grow and harvest enough vegetables for a family of four. Since the preparation of the soil had been done by the Mylora crew, planting, weeding and harvesting constituted the main chores. Many planned on growing some of the more difficult species during the next growing season. The knowledge that 120 more converts to nutritious, poison-free food and a cleaner environment had taken their basic training in the organically balanced soil at Mylora has been a source of deep, personal satisfaction to me.

To help you to adapt our allotment plan to your own garden our planting schedules are given in detail in this chapter but because there are exceptions to every rule and because farming demands flexibility, the following comments should be kept in mind.

TIMES OF PLANTING

Timing is always a critical factor in obtaining optimum germination. The dates set forth in the planting charts are predicated on our experience at Mylora which is located on the forty-ninth parallel of latitude, at sea level and well-protected from prevailing winds. Another area which might be located in a hollow or on a windy hilltop will require an adjustment of several days from our own dates.

Edwin F. Steffek in *Gardening the Easy Way* suggests a useful formula; the season regresses about a hundred miles a week for each additional degree of latitude from the equator and about ten days for each additional thousand feet of altitude. Conversely, the planting dates would be advanced. Thus, if you are closer to the pole than to the forty-ninth parallel, above sea level and facing the ocean, you will have three reasons to delay your planting and all three must be added together in determining how much later you should plant.

If you are unsure of your calculations, it is always wise to ask an experienced gardener in your area for safe planting times.

Even in as comparatively small a holding as Mylora, we have observed dramatic differences in timing. Bisected as it is by a north-south freeway, Mylora can be visualized as being made up of an eastern and a western half. The western fields lie between the freeway and a housing subdivision, while the eastern half is quite open with only a few houses scattered on the periphery. We have learned to depend on strawberries planted west of the freeway ripening three days ahead of those growing in the eastern fields. On the eastern fields we have also experienced spotty damage in tomatoes by unseasonable July frosts.

SEEDING

Buying seeds in attractive packages is usually more expensive than buying in bulk; furthermore it is difficult to estimate the number of seeds that are in a sealed seed package.

If you have any seed remaining from the previous year, it should be planted more thickly since the percentage of seeds which will germinate diminishes with time. Some gardeners add the old seed to the new and plant this mixture a little more thickly. They feel that it is safer because it is possible that the seed you purchase might have been already stored for several seasons. The depths indicated on the charts apply to Mylora soil which is a heavy clay and very cold in a wet spring. The three main factors that determine the planting depth are the size of the seed itself, the time of the year it is to be planted, and the moisture present in the soil at the time the seed is introduced. You must bear in mind that a tiny seed will not be able to push through too much soil; that the seed must not dry out during the germination process, and that during warmer weather, the soil will dry out from the top down.

THE PLAN ITSELF

The plan embraces four plantings so as to provide continuing harvests throughout the season. It is designed to take advantage of the symbiotic effects that occur between different families of plants, and is limited to the plants which have proven easiest to grow. The absence of such common vegetables as cabbage, cauliflower, turnips and broccoli from the charts is explained by the particular growing conditions each requires so that these are dealt with elsewhere in this book. Because the plan is merely an introduction to organic farming, I felt it wiser to omit the more temperamental crops that attract insects and disease until the environment is completely suitable. I suggest that only small areas of these vegetables be planted before large scale cultivation is attempted.

SOIL

Building up your soil as a protection against insects and disease can be done at any time of the year that is convenient. A compost heap can be started now; compost or manure can be added to the garden anytime. Should it be incompletely decayed, it must be placed on the surface but if it is properly decayed, rototiller, rakes and hoes can all be used to incorporate it into the surface soil. During the growing season, it may be placed between rows of plants.

Some plants thrive anywhere at Mylora but certain species such as carrots, beans and raspberries grow considerably better in light soil. The majority, however, including strawberries, potatoes, broadbeans, beets, parsnips, tomatoes, and all the cole crops prefer heavy soil. Peas, corn, squash, lettuce and onions grow equally well in the heavy or light soil.

BIOLOGICALLY SAFE INSECT CONTROLS

The organic farmer must never allow himself to depend on any pesticide or unnatural form of insect control. It is sometimes tempting when you are desperate and when you want to co-operate with a regional control programme to make a temporary pact with the devil. A short-term success can weaken the resolution and you may become dependent on chemicals and finish in the same situation as commercial farmers. Biological control is the only safe method, so experiment and study natural techniques.

The garden hose can be an effective insect control when it is used knowledgeably. Lack of moisture can so weaken a plant that it will attract insects. The addition of moisture makes the plant healthy so that it grows at its optimum rate and insects will not be attracted to it. This very simple solution seems too easy to be credible to many, but moisture distribution has been constantly stressed in these pages because it is at the very core of successful organic farming.

A more dramatic method of repelling insect pests is by the planting of such strongly aromatic herbs as sage, thyme or rosemary among food crops. Flowers that either by their fragrance or symbiotic relationships at the root level seem to serve the same purpose are nasturtiums and marigolds.

We experimented in polyculture by planting alternate rows of beets and cabbages and were richly rewarded with the vigorous growth of both vegetables. The beets did especially well, and a comparison with another field in which the beets were grown monoculturally showed that the tops of the beets grown among the cabbages were markedly superior. Although we cannot answer the questions about the protein carbohydrate ratio or the mineral content the flavour test indicated good quality. We are still wondering whether this success was due to a symbiotic factor relating to sunlight. In polyculture, the taller growing plants receive the full sunlight on the upper surfaces of their leaves and the upper part of the stem only. The lower area of the stem as well as the soil at the base of the stem is shaded by the lower growing plants. In our experiment, the lower growing plants, the beets,

TOOLS

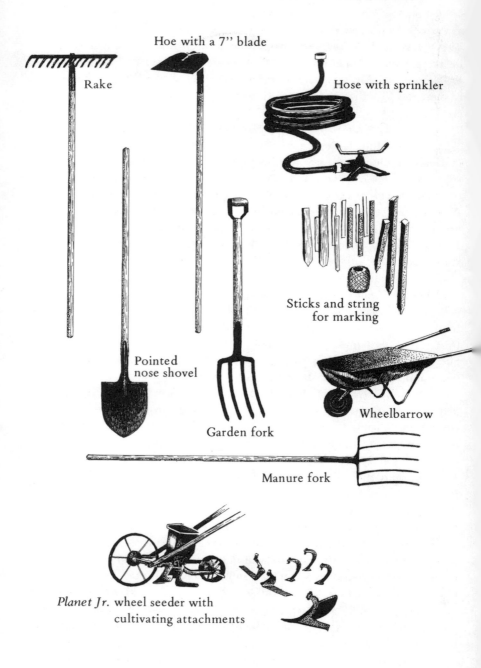

Rake

Hoe with a 7'' blade

Hose with sprinkler

Pointed
nose shovel

Garden fork

Sticks and string
for marking

Wheelbarrow

Manure fork

Planet Jr. wheel seeder with
cultivating attachments

received their sunlight filtered through the leaves of the taller cabbage plants. Previously we believed that food plants must have all the sunlight possible on every part of their foliage. Now we wonder.

WORKING YOUR PLOT

Experienced gardeners and farmers will find the following section elementary, yet, as I have learned from Mylora's "Grow Your Own Organic Produce" project, it is the young people who are most receptive to the principles of organic farming, yet they usually have no gardening experience whatsoever.

Tools

Garden rake	Hoe with seven inch blade	Spading fork
Point nosed shovel	Garden hose and sprinkler	Sticks and strings
If you are able to obtain some manure —		for marking
Wheelbarrow and manure fork		

For a large garden you will also need a rototiller unless you are able to rent one. A combination hand seed planter with attachments for cultivating will also expedite your work.

If you have a large area and livestock are permissible in your district, the manure will be a prime activator for your compost piles. Even a few chickens will turn surplus vegetation and discarded table waste into superb poultry and eggs.

Winter — Planning

During the winter, plan the garden carefully using graph paper. Make a realistic assessment of the amount of food you will need from your garden.

Plan for less rather than more, so that you can give your garden adequate care.

Do not use all your land merely because it is available. It is far better to grow fewer vegetables that offer superior nutrition than great quantities of poor quality fare.

Unused land with the addition of organic waste material can be left to build itself up in preparation for subsequent growing seasons.

Choose suitable types of vegetables for your family's taste. Change the proportions on the charts if you wish, but do not depart from it radically until you are more experienced. If you have had trouble growing a particular vegetable eliminate it and plant more of the others.

Do not be misled by glowing illustrations and promises on seed packages. The old tried and true varieties are almost always hardier and usually give better all-round results.

SUBSOILING

1) Expose a section of subsoil by placing it to one side of the area to be dug.
2) Loosen exposed subsoil with a shovel.
3) Remove an adjacent section of topsoil and place it on the already loosened subsoil.
4-7) Repeat the process until the entire area is worked.

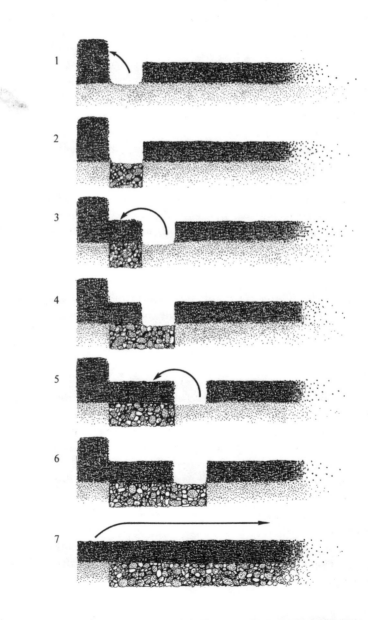

Late Winter — Preparing the Soil

To increase the fertility of your soil, add compost, manure, rotted straw, hay, seaweed or any other organic material.

Cut up the sod (the top layer of grass) together with about an inch or so of earth using a sharp spade or a powered rototiller. An alternative method is to remove the sod, stacking it neatly in a corner to decay, from whence it can be returned to the garden as an enriching soil-builder during the next growing season. The earth which is removed with the sod must be kept to an absolute minimum because this is the most fertile part of your garden soil.

Remove a shovelful or two to determine the depth of your top soil. An abrupt change in the texture and colour will indicate the line between the subsoil and the topsoil.

Should there be any indications that the subsoil is compacted, i.e., that it is hard and impervious, or should there be any evidence that plant roots have been growing laterally against the subsoil instead of penetrating in to it, the subsoil should be loosened.

Never further compact your soil by unnecessary walking on the areas that have been loosened, especially if it is wet.

Early Spring

When the topsoil is dry enough to break or shatter, loosen it down to the subsoil. A shovel pushed through the topsoil will loosen it sufficiently when the handle is pulled back a little. Should the soil squeeze like putty instead of breaking or crumbling, it is too wet and will need more time to dry out. Working wet soil is difficult and destructive and you are better to allow further drying before re-working. Heavy clay soils, in the process of drying out, go through a stage at which the lumps shatter easily, and for best results you should watch for this stage and work the soil when it is reached. Each time you work the soil you bring wet soil from below the surface. Allow this wet soil to dry before working it further.

When the surface has dried sufficiently, a hoe or rake is quite satisfactory to break up the lumps. A light, chopping action does the job efficiently.

Continue smoothing out the soil until the lumps approximate the size of the seed to be planted.

If you can wait until the first weed seeds germinate in your newly smoothed soil before planting your seeds, two advantages will accrue: germinating weeds will be easily killed with the rake or hoe as you are sowing, and the soil will be warmer so that your vegetables will germinate and grow more rapidly, while fewer will fail to germinate.

Early Spring — Seeding

Make a straight line parallel to the north-south boundary of the garden. A string stretched between two sticks in the soil provides a satisfactory guide.

With the handle of the hoe, make a furrow along the line of the string at the depth suggested in CHART FOR FIRST PLANTING page 100, for the seed to be sown.

Consult the charts again for the distance required between the plants when they are fully grown. You will need to plant three or four times as many of the fine seeds as has been suggested for mature plants. Extra seedlings will eventually be thinned out. Even though seeds fall at various angles into the furrow, the roots always grow downwards and the stem upwards as they germinate. It is necessary to be careful when dropping fine seed such as lettuce, carrots, onions etc. Should too many of these fall into one spot in the seed furrow it will be impossible to pick them up singly. Rather than leave them in this cluster, scoop out a handful of earth with the seeds and scatter the mixture of earth and seeds along the furrow.

Crowded seedlings will be spindly since they will be competing with one another for soil, moisture and air. Furthermore, the thinning out process is very apt to damage those left behind, so a careful sowing and spacing saves future headaches.

If you have never planted fine seeds before, it will be worth your while to practise doing so. Take a pinch of seeds between the thumb and first two fingers and by moving the thumb slightly, practise dropping them back into the original package until you feel you have control over their fall.

In windy weather, take care that the fine seeds do not blow away from, rather than into, the furrow.

When planting in dry weather, make sure that the time between opening the furrow and covering the seed is as short as possible. This is essential to conserve precious moisture.

Cover the seed to the correct depth according to the charts and rake the surface above the seed smooth and free of lumps.

Hold the handle of the rake vertically so that the tines rest on the soil surface. Pat the soil gently all along the surface of the seed furrow with the flat of the tines.

Proceed until you have the whole row completed, then consult the chart for the space between the rows and complete all rows in CHART FOR FIRST PLANTING. each with its appropriate seeds.

Mark the row of seeds with a named tag.

Immediately prepare and smooth a further garden area for the next planting, (see CHART FOR SECOND PLANTING, page 101) to encourage germination of weed seeds in that area.

Consult the CHART FOR FIRST PLANTING for the approximate time of emergence for the first seedlings.

Do not walk on the planted area until you can see the rows of emerging seedlings. You will then know just where to place your feet as you work the soil.

The novice may experience difficulty in recognizing vegetable seedlings as opposed to weed seedlings which emerge at the same time. However, the straight rows of the planted seedlings can be relied upon to determine the location of the rows. You will then be able to hoe the area between them.

Early May

When you see these lines of seedlings in the first planting it is time to proceed with the second planting and subsequently to prepare the soil for the third sowing.

As soon as the soil is prepared for the third seeding the earth which has been hilled up over the potatoes (see CHART FOR FIRST PLANTING) should be carefully levelled with the rake. Explore the newly uncovered soil with your fingers looking for sprouts from the potato seeds and observe and note their length, being careful not to break the sprouts nor to disturb the seed. Remake the hill in exactly the same place again. If you are not exact in remaking the hill you may inadvertently damage some potato seed or sprouts.

Repeat the process about every five days until the sprouts are long enough to emerge through the level soil. Do not remake the hill but leave the soil level. The hilling and raking should control weeds effectively.

The first two leaves of a seedling sometimes have characteristics which differ from all subsequent leaves the plant will grow. To avoid making an error, it is wise not to attempt to weed or thin out until you are absolutely certain that you can differentiate between the seedlings you have planted and the unwelcome weed seedlings. We suggest, therefore, that when in doubt you should wait until the seedlings have produced at least four leaves and have developed their definite characteristics. As soon as you are sure remove all the weeds.

When weeds which you did not remove the first time because either they had not germinated or they were too small to see have grown about three-quarters as high as the vegetables, it is time for the second weeding and thinning. If the plants are thinned so as to leave twice as many as needed, then should you damage some of the young plants, there are sufficient remaining to provide a good crop, and the

THE IDENTIFICATION OF SEEDLINGS

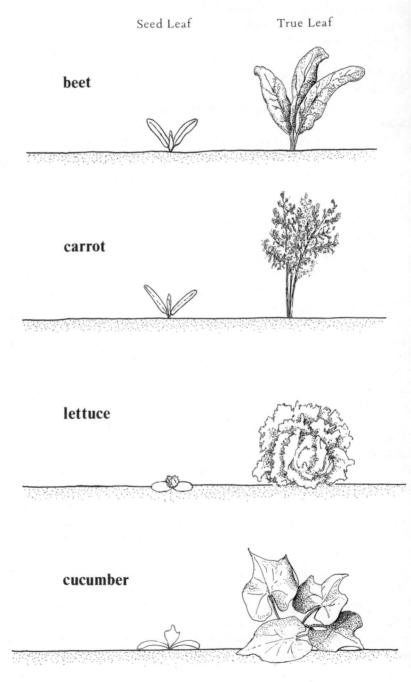

Seed Leaf   True Leaf

beet

carrot

lettuce

cucumber

vegetable seedlings which you will pull out later will be large enough for eating. Be sure however that the final thinning is done before the leaves of adjacent plants begin to crowd one another.

After this thinning and weeding, pull the soil gently up and around the stems of almost all of the plants by using the hand or hoe. Some of the lower leaves of the plants may be covered with soil, but those on top must always remain exposed to the sunlight. This process is called "hilling" and it encourages the plant roots to invade the very rich area which was formerly surface soil and has just now been covered. Hilling also smothers tiny weed seedlings which may germinate close to the stems of the plants and would otherwise be quite difficult to remove. Both beets and lettuce should be hilled only very lightly, whereas onions must not be hilled at all or they will develop thick necks.

If the potatoes are six to nine inches high they can be well hilled up.

Carry on with the third planting according to the directions of the chart, and prepare the soil for the next sowing.

Remove any weeds that have been missed, but once food plants shade all the underlying soil any small weeds that are shaded can be ignored.

At all times, maintain a loose, friable soil between the rows by hoeing gently. Always remember that the purpose of this procedure is to keep a soft mulch on the surface and be careful not to hoe too deeply since root damage is almost certain to occur. Compacted soil invites problems. We have had experience of rust fly infestation along rows of carrots where the soil was first compacted by too much foot traffic accompanied by heavy rains.

Late May — Watering

Watch soil moisture content during hot, dry weather. Coarse sandy soils dry out much more rapidly than fine clay soils, and insect attacks will result.

An illustration of the results of dry soil on a tomato crop at Mylora may help to explain the importance of moisture so that new gardeners can be spared our costly education in this matter. The simple error of using dry, rather than moist, earth to cover the roots of tomatoes as they were being set out in the field first impeded their growth and, as the weather remained warm and dry for several weeks, flea beetles moved in on the weakened plants and almost destroyed them. We did not realize what the problem was until after the rains came. The moisture caused the plants to revive almost miraculously and since the plants now grew at optimum rate the aphids disappeared. Although from that time the plants did well, the harvest was a disappointment because the plants could not make up for the early setback that bad planting had caused.

The best time for watering the garden is in the early morning. The soil will then have a chance to warm up after being chilled by the water and the leaves can dry off during the heat of the day. Evening waterings of such crops as potatoes or beans encourage the development of fungus diseases by prolonging the moisture on both soil and plant leaves.

Soils vary in the rate at which they can absorb moisture so apply the water at no greater rate than the soil can absorb it. If too much is being applied the soil will become packed and the water will run to the low spots carrying some of the topsoil with it.

Sometimes it takes twenty-four hours for moisture to become thoroughly dispersed throughout the soil. Therefore allow this time to elapse before adding more. Make sure that there is not a layer of dry soil between the newly moistened surface soil and the moisture in the lower part of the topsoil, otherwise the surface moisture will evaporate rapidly. When the surface has dried after irrigation loosen it with a hoe and make a dust mulch to conserve the moisture you have just applied.

The determined organic gardener will not allow spaces in the garden to remain empty and bare no matter whether the space was caused by an early harvest, insect damaged plants or poor germination. Such areas must at least be encouraged to grow weeds — kept neatly trimmed if you wish — or planted to a soil improving crop, such as fall rye. We take advantage of all the growing season to plant vegetables which will mature later in the year. We are, however, always careful not to plant long growing varieties late in the season. Keep the hose, garden rake, hoe and seeds ready. DO NOT wait till the entire row is empty but plant each small area as it becomes available. The latest dates at which we seed the various kinds of vegetables are:

FINAL PLANTING DATES

June 1	Mid season corn	Vetch's Autumn Giant cauliflower
June 15	Early cabbage	Early peas
July 1	Carrots	Broccoli
July 15	Green & Wax bush beans	Green onions
Aug. 1	Head lettuce	
Aug. 15	Leaf lettuce	
Sept. 1	Chinese cabbage	

Harvesting

Carrots, beets, onions, lettuce and potatoes can be eaten at any time during their growth.

Peas should be picked when the pods are filled and before they begin to show any lighter colouring along the edge of the pod. This fading of the colour of the pod happens simultaneously with the hardening of the peas and a loss of sweetness. When cooked at this stage they can be still enjoyed.

Beans should be eaten when they are four to five inches long but before the seeds inside have developed sufficiently to show their position in the pod.

Cucumbers: lighter colouring on the skin of cucumbers occurs when the cucumber is changing from growth to seed development resulting in a loss of succulence. The flavour and crispness is best when the skin is dark green.

Summer squash such as vegetable marrow, zucchini, and patty pan can be eaten at any time during the growing season, but if they are to be stored, you must let them mature on the vine until the skin is tough enough to resist the pressure of the thumbnail. Winter squashes are not usually harvested until they are fully mature and will keep in prime condition for many months.

Corn can be picked when the kernels on the cob have developed fully all along its length to the tip. You can determine this by firmly squeezing the middle of the cob between the thumb and forefinger and running the pressure along to the tip. If the cob is fully formed right to the tip, open the tip of the husk and have a look at the kernels. If they have not yet filled out, cover them again with the husk and leave the cob on the stalk to mature further. Should this test cob be ready for picking, take note of the dryness of the tassel silks at the tip of the cob, and using this as a guide you can judge which of the other cobs are ready for harvesting without the necessity of opening the husks. Insects sometimes attack the kernels of corn once the husks have been opened.

Onions must have their necks, roots, and outer skins thoroughly dried before they are put into storage to ensure good keeping quality.

Winter potatoes must have skins that are firm enough so that they cannot be easily rubbed off; storage life will be shortened considerably if the skins are not hardened.

We have been able to control scab on potatoes, which shows up at harvest time, by growing red clover for two years on our heavier type of soil before planting.

Carrots are better left growing in the soil as late as possible providing that there is no danger of heavy frost or rust fly infestation.

The fall rains will make them more succulent and they will retain their crispness for a longer period during the winter months. One year they were so badly infested that we had to discard the major part of them. It would appear to us that the rust fly maggots were in the soil but did not attack the carrots since they were growing vigorously. It could be argued that the maggots hatched out later than usual in October but since the weather was cold and wet we do not think this was the case. It is the first time we had such an experience.

It is important to remember that harvested vegetables are still living, so that during storage they give off moisture and heat. Satisfactory storage slows down their rate of living thus prolonging their life and nutritive qualities.

After harvesting, all soil surfaces must be protected against the damaging effect of winter rains. Either allow a ground cover of weeds and grass to develop or cover garden areas with an organic mulch. Alternatively plant fall rye or winter wheat, preferably before September fifteenth. Although it will grow if planted later, the heavy frosts may heave it out of the soil so that the crop offers little protection.

Crop rotation plays an important role in the polycultural system of growing. The simplest way to accomplish this is to plant the garden each year from the other end.

FOR COMMERCIAL FARMERS

Some farmers, particularly livestock producers, have not introduced many chemicals into their soil. With the addition of manure and careful cultivation their soils have become more productive and their insect and disease problems are minimal. They are in reality practicing many principles of the organic concept in their farming techniques.

Others have memories of their earlier days when they grew good crops with far fewer insect and disease problems than today. They know that present farming methods with the resulting chemical contamination of the environment are worsening the situation yet they fear to change because of the financial risks involved.

Realizing the difficulties of a sudden and complete changeover from chemical to biological farming, I make some suggestions which allow the grower to test organic principles in a limited but a progressive way. These suggestions have the advantage that they involve farm management rather than the expenditure of large sums of money.

1) Dedicate some spare land to the future and help it to refurbish itself. This area should be selected so that it will be subject neither to drifting sprays from adjoining fields nor to drainage from soils containing chemicals which could contaminate it.

2) If you feel that you cannot spare the land you might consider cutting down the area of crops which are only marginally profitable or those which require large amounts of pesticides and/or herbicides. Alternatively you might be able to rent land and use it to grow income producing crops while you organically revitalize your own dedicated area.

3) Till with the subsoiler the dedicated area and plant it to deep rooted legumes and grasses. A wide variety of both early and late maturing species will maintain the growth over a longer period of time, thus increasing the total organic content.

4) As the sod is developing, mow the field regularly. The energy of the plants will be directed into leaf growth rather than seed development. As the clippings fall to the ground they add to the organic content of the soil.

5) If livestock is available the area could be stocked lightly during the second year or grazed moderately heavily for very short periods of time. The droppings of the livestock must be spread around with a drag harrow.

6) Be constantly on the lookout for any organic material which you can obtain cheaply and spread it on the area whenever it becomes available.

7) Rather than using herbicides in row crops try to develop mechanical techniques for weed control. With a little thought and ingenuity you will discover many different ways for doing so. Discuss mechanical weed control with older farmers for in the old days before herbicides, when they grew small grains, peas, potatoes, etc., they had to develop effective mechanical techniques for weed control. The practise of hilling up and knocking down rows of potatoes to control weeds can be applied to most row crops but it takes ingenuity and perseverance, essential qualities for any farmer.

8) Saturate your mind with reading material on the subject of organic growing and develop the habit of thinking out your problems biologically rather than chemically.

9) If damaging insects show up in your crop do not be in too much hurry to destroy them. Look first to see if their natural predators are present in sufficient numbers and if so give them a little time to effect control.

10) Do not take out all the natural weed growth on the boundaries or along ditches for the sake of tidiness. This growth could be neatly trimmed for appearance. Trees, brush and scrub hold the banks of ditches against collapse and are necessary for habitation of predator and parasitic types of insects as well as birds, frogs, snakes and the various forms of life which maintain the natural balance so vital

THE GARDEN PLAN

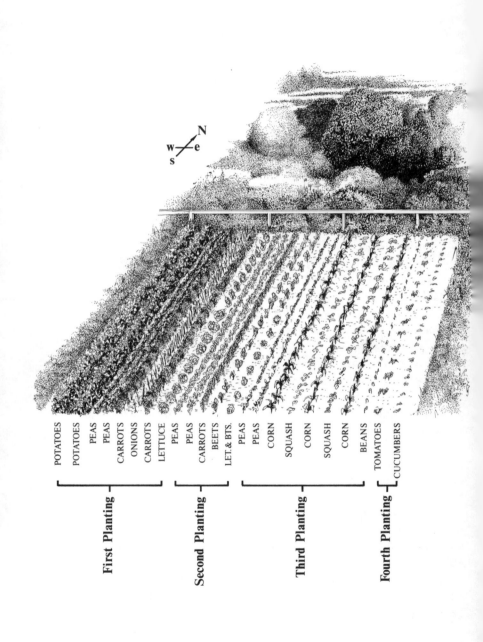

First Planting: POTATOES, POTATOES, PEAS, PEAS, CARROTS, ONIONS, CARROTS, LETTUCE

Second Planting: PEAS, PEAS, CARROTS, BEETS, LET. & BTS.

Third Planting: PEAS, PEAS, CORN, SQUASH, CORN, SQUASH, CORN, BEANS

Fourth Planting: TOMATOES, CUCUMBERS

o life.

11) Strip cropping rather than planting entire fields assists natural insect and disease control and at the same time contributes toward polyculture provided that the strips are not too wide.

12) A three year old sod should give you a fairly good basis to start organic growing. Commence with your least troublesome crops. When the soil becomes richer and you have had more experience attempt small quantities of the more troublesome types of crops.

13) If it is not practical to seed a cover crop for winter soil protection, then scatter clover seed among the growing plants after the last weeding in spring. Summer rains will germinate them and provide a little extra protection for the winter with an excellent soil building potential, if the field is not to be planted the following year.

14) Remember that there are no half measures in organic growing. Chemicals added to the soil can damage the forms of life you are struggling to encourage. Do not defeat your purpose.

15) Time is the limiting factor in building up the soil biologically for large populations of various organisms have to increase. This process will be fostered by the addition of adequate organic matter.

16) Should you have a fund set aside for your organic project, do not be tempted to spend it on artificial plant food to force growth; rather spend the money on manures or any suitable organic material you can purchase reasonably and spread it on your soil whenever it becomes available regardless of the time of the year.

17) When you begin to till your dedicated area again, sheet composting is an easy and effective way of increasing the fertility which you have been building up. The value of compost lies not in its chemical components but in the multiplicity of micro-organisms and their products and by-products.

The method we use at Mylora is very simple. The stubble or other green material left after harvesting is covered first with a spreading of manure on the surface and subsequently covered if possible with a light layer of soil by means of heavy harrows to prevent the manure from drying out. If it is not too late in the season the heat and moisture should be sufficient to encourage bacteria to work and a winter cover crop to flourish. Such composting will be successful in stimulating the necessary biological action that is the basis of fertility.

THE GARDEN PLAN

The suggested twenty-three rows with 15 - 22 inch spacings require approximately 42 feet with a suggested length of 20 feet. These measurements provide an area of approximately 850 square feet of planted garden, about one fiftieth of an acre which is 43,560 sq. ft. or

4840 sq. yds., say 70 yds. x 70 yds.

In the allotments last year we used twelve and eighteen inch spacings between rows. While this spacing was adequate for the smaller plants such as carrots, it was a little close for inexperienced gardeners to work with and so we suggest a wider spacing here. But we recommend closer spacing in subsequent plantings.

CHART FOR FIRST PLANTING (A)

Crop	Depth of seed	Space between mature plants	Distance to next row	Planting time	Expected time of emergence in weeks
Potatoes	1½"	10"	22"	15 April	3–4
Potatoes	1½	10	22	15 April	3–4
Peas	1	¾	15	15 April	2–3
Peas	1	¾	15	15 April	2–3
Carrots	½	¾	15	15 April	2–3
Onions	½	¾	15	15 April	2–4
Carrots	½	¾	15	15 April	2–3
Lettuce	¼	12	15	15 April	1½–2½

1) In sowing the smaller seeds such as onions, lettuce etc., use about three or four times as many seeds as the chart suggests for mature plants. The extra seedlings can be thinned out later.

2) We suggest half a row of leaf lettuce and half a row of head lettuce. The variation in the times necessary for maturity will spread out the harvesting time so giving you a continuous supply of lettuce over a longer period.

3) Space the peas carefully. They are better not thinned out.

4) The depth of the potato seed is measured from the top of the seed piece of potato carrying the eye. After the potatoes are planted the earth should be hilled over the row about two inches above the general soil level.

5) The time of expected emergence of seedlings varies with the soil temperatures and types of soil but should approximate the time suggested.

6) The peas are planted in adjacent rows and must be encouraged to become entwined with one another so that they do not fall on top of the neighbouring rows of other plants. Hill up adjacent rows of peas so that they fall towards each other.

7) A guide to the approximate number of seeds per ounce is as follows:

Lettuce, carrots and parsley   22,000

Turnips, parsnips, onions and broccoli	10,000
Radishes and beets	1,700
Cucumber	800
Bush-beans, corn, pumpkins and squash	100 - 300
Pole-beans	50

CHART FOR SECOND PLANTING (B)

Crop	Depth of seed	Space between mature plants	Distance to next row	Planting time
Peas	1 "	¾"	15"	1 May
Peas	1	¾	15	1 May
Carrots	½	¾	15	1 May
Beets	½	¾	15	1 May
Lettuce & beets	½	12	15	1 May

For this planting we suggest one-half row of beets and one-half row of head lettuce. The time of emergence of the seedlings will be less because the soil will be warmer.

CHART FOR THIRD PLANTING (C)

Crop	Depth of seed	Space between mature plants	Distance to next row	Planting time
Peas	1½"	¾ "	15"	15 May
Peas	1½	¾	15	15 May
Corn	1½	10	22	15 May
Squash	1½	10	22	15 May
Corn	1½	10	22	15 May
Squash	1½	10	22	15 May
Corn	1½	10	22	15 May
Beans	1½	1	15	15 May

Three quarters of a row of green and one-quarter of a row of golden butter beans provides a delightful variety. At this later date the soil is warmer and the seeds will germinate even more rapidly.

CHART FOR FOURTH PLANTING (D)

Crop	Depth of seed	Space between mature plants	Distance to next row	Planting time
Tomato plants	on the surface	22"	22"	22 May
Cucumbers	1½"	6	22	30 May

You may like to try some of the crops we find more difficult to grow in our area. The following will help you:

CHART FOR EXTRA PLANTING (E)

Crop	Depth of seed	Space between mature plants	Distance to next row	Planting time
Broadbeans	2½"	15"	22"	Late March
Parsley	½	12	15	Early April
Wheat	1	½	6	1–10 May
Oats	¾	½	6	1–10 May
Parsnips	1	2	15	20 May
Early Cabbage	1	12	15	20 May
Late Red	1	22	22	20 May
Savoy Cabbage	1	22	22	20 May
Early Broccoli	1	22	22	20 May
Late Cauliflower	1	22	22	20 May
Late Broccoli	1	22	22	1 June
Swede Turnips	1	12	15	1 June
Chinese Cabbage	1	12	15	Late August
Fall Rye	1½	½	6	Early September

Parsley takes a long time to germinate. The seeds are very small and therefore must be planted near the surface. In order to prevent the soil drying out before germination occurs place some old sacks over the seeded soil until the seedlings emerge.

SMALL FRUITS
Strawberries

Strawberries are a tricky crop which we plant early in the second week of May. They vary considerably in their growth patterns from one area to another so it will be helpful to find an experienced grower among your neighbours to learn what may be expected. Reserve the richest part of the garden for them and be sure the area is well drained. In the Pacific Northwest they spend the first year making growth to produce fruit in the following season. A good-sized plant with a number of crowns, the central woody stem part of the plant between the roots and the leaves, may be developed or alternatively, many small runner plants, depending on which system of culture is chosen. If the former, place the plants 12 - 15 inches apart and keep the runner plants cut as fast as they develop. The alternative method necessitates spacing the plants 40 inches apart and encouraging the runners to take root by arranging them carefully and anchoring them in place with some soil so they can develop roots as they run. Whichever method is used, removing the blossoms from the plants during the first year is said to strengthen and encourage the plant to survive the dangerous winter ahead and set an adequate amount of fruit for the following season. Unfortunately, strawberries sometimes fail to survive the winter due to freezing, suffocation from too much water or infection by root diseases. They may be eaten by mice or moles who also appear to have a craving for the crowns of the plants.

If you are concerned because of the high winter mortality rate of strawberry plants, you can use some new varieties which have been developed which will fruit late in July following planting. They do not have the full-blown flavour of the standard variety, but at least you will have some crop to justify your efforts before the plants face winterkill. If you are lucky and the plants survive the winter you will have berries in the following spring as well. One winter hazard to strawberry plants is the height of the water table. This should never be closer to the soil surface than 18 inches.

The precautions we take at Mylora against the Red Stele organism are to plant the strawberries in the richest soil available.

Use only good plants, preferably those which are dug during dormancy and held in cold storage until planting time.

When the soil is thoroughly warm transplant them according to the hilling system spacing plants 12 - 15 inches apart.

Remove blossoms as they develop, keep the weeds checked, and remove the runners as they appear. At the end of the summer see that the drainage ditch which must surround the fields is about 18 inches deep. We also dig ditches at 100 foot intervals throughout the field. The soil between the rows should be opened up with a subsoiler to allow drainage after the compaction which occurs during the summer.

Only the extreme top of the crown and the leaves —if any—should remain exposed to the sunlight after planting. The roots should be straight and well fanned out in the soil. The soil must be made unusually firm around the roots. We suggest the eighth of May as a good planting time. We have grown over 25 different varieties in an attempt to overcome the Red Stele problems. For a number of years the Siletz variety grew well but it no longer grows satisfactorily so we recommend Cheam or Totem.

Raspberries

Raspberries should be set out in the fall. A spacing of 2½ - 3 feet between plants in the row is usual and as in all planting and transplantings, extreme care must be taken to tamp the earth firmly over the roots so as to exclude all air.

SOME COMMON TYPES OF SQUASH

Zucchini

Pumpkin

Blue Hubbard

Green Hubbard

Acorn

Butternut

White Vegetable Marrow

Buttercup

Green Delicious

Golden Hubbard

Set the canes in the soil so that their former rooting area (all the parts of the roots which were in the ground) is completely covered.

VARIETIES GROWN AT MYLORA

The following is a list of named varieties which we have grown satisfactorily at Mylora.

Kind	Type	Variety, 1st Choice	2nd Choice
Beans	Green bush	Tendercrop	Pearl Green
Beans	Butter or Wax	Pure Gold	
Beans	Pole	Bluelake	
Beans	Pole	Romano	
Beets	All Seasons	Greentop Bunching	
Broadbeans		Exhibition Long Pod	
Broccoli	Early & Late	Italian Green Sprouting	
Cabbage	Early Green	Jersey Wakefield	
Cabbage	Late Green	Houston Evergreen, Siedl	
		Danish Ballhead	
Cabbage	Savoy	Chieftain	
Cabbage	Late Red	Mammoth Red Rock	
Carrots	Medium	Nantes	
Cauliflower	Late	Vetch's Autumn Giant	
Corn	Early	Early King	
Corn	Mid-season	Golden Bantam	
Corn	Late	F.M.Cross	
Cucumbers	Slicing	Marketer	
Cucumbers	Pickling	Ohio M.R. 17	
Lettuce	Leaf	Grand Rapids	
Lettuce	Head	Valverde	
Oats	Spring	Eagle	
Onions	Green	White Lisbon	
Onions	Dry	Autumn Spice	
Parsley		Triple Moss Curled	
Parsnips		Hollow Crown	
Peas	Early	Laxton Progress #9	
Peas	Late	Onward	
Potatoes	Mid-season	Red Pontiac	
Raspberries		Willamette	Fairview
Rye	Fall	Tetra Petkus	
Strawberries	Main Crop	Cheam, Totem	Siletz
Strawberries	Everbearing	Quinault	Red Rich
Tomato	Bush	Starfire	Fireball
Turnips	Swede	Laurentian	
Wheat	Spring	Thatcher	

THE COMPOST BOX

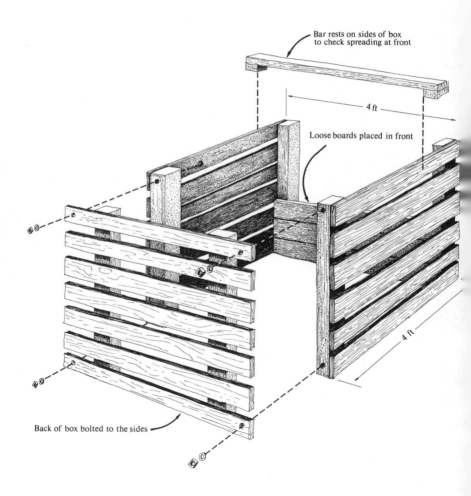

Bar rests on sides of box
to check spreading at front

4 ft

Loose boards placed in front

4 ft

Back of box bolted to the sides

Squash: We grow most of the varieties of squash but
they vary so much in flavour that we hesitate
to recommend one more than another.

"Autumn Spice", a variety of onions, serves the two purposes of
dry and green onions. Use the thinnings as green onions and leave the
balance to mature and dry thoroughly for winter keeping.

The list includes some of the newer hybrids. All these have grown
well and vigorously at Mylora except pickling cucumbers.

HOUSEHOLD COMPOST

Household waste becomes garden wealth when made into compost. Even the waste from a small household will produce good compost.

You must be careful to exclude any poisonous substances from
your compost.

Construct a box, fastened together with bolts so that it can be
dismantled, about four feet wide by four feet long and three feet high.
The wood should be coated with a natural preservative such as linseed
oil to lengthen its life. The sides of the box must be slatted to allow
free air access. No bottom is necessary since the compost must come
into direct contact with fertile soil — not sod — to facilitate the
interaction between the organisms in the soil and the compost.

As the daily refuse is put into the box some dry soil is sprinkled
over the surface. A pile of loose dry earth protected from the rain
should be handy. The earth assists composting and prevents odours.
When a six inch layer of waste has accumulated an eighth of an inch
sprinkling of a protein rich substance such as meat-meal, blood-meal or
fish-meal is added to provide the activity for composting. If manure —
which is preferable — is available, about a two inch layer is required.

While building the pile keep the material loose by gently forking
the top layer with each addition. Do not press down on the pile.
A stout upright stick should be placed in the middle of the box during
the building. When the box is full the stick is removed and the hole left
to provide ventilation. At all times the pile should be prevented from
becoming too moist or too dry by providing protection against the sun,
rain and wind. The moisture content must be continuously maintained
to the consistency of a wrung out sponge. In warm dry weather the pile
may need a frequent light sprinkling with a watering can.

Should the pile become smelly or attract flies, it could be too wet or
too dry and the material should be re-mixed. If the box is almost full
it may be easier to unbolt the box and move it to another position than
to repile the materials and adjust the moisture content.

When the box is filled to the top it should be covered and the
compost allowed to ripen until it is friable and sweet smelling. The

time it takes varies according to the weather. If it is repiled after cooling down, the ripening process is accelerated.

If the compost cannot be spread as soon as it is ripe it should be completely protected by covering it with a film of plastic until needed.

When the compost is spread over the garden it must be raked or forked into the soil immediately. This should be done on a cool damp day so that the compost does not dry out.

Bibliography

Suggested readings in the philosophy and practice of Organic Farming.

Pleasant Valley   Louis Bromfield   *Harper*
Malabar Farm
>   Delightful introductions to organic farming as practised in two separate locations. Contains many practical applications of the organic way and is pervaded with a sincere reverence for life at every level.

The Soil and Health   Sir Albert Howard   *Devin, Adair*
An Agricultural Testament   *Faber and Faber*
Farming and Gardening   *Oxford University*
*   for Health or Disease*   *Press*
>   The scientific and philosophical writings of the founder of the organic farming movement. As relevant today as when first published.

Pay Dirt   J.I. Rodale   *Devin, Adair*
The Living Soil   Eve Balfour   *Faber and Faber*
>   Both offer a complete insight into the miraculous and busy life of the soil.

Silent Spring   Rachel Carson   *Houghton-Mifflin*
>   The first, dramatic warning of the delayed costs of our chemically-saturated environment.

Since Silent Spring   Frank Graham, Jr.   *Fawcett; Crest Books*
>   Documentation of the events and attitudes of the public, the scientific community, and certain officials of government after the initial impact of Rachel Carson's work.

Restoring the Quality   President's Science   *U.S. Department*
*   of our Environment*   Advisory Committee   *of Documents*
>   A report requested by the late President, John F. Kennedy after he read "Silent Spring". It is being hustled into oblivion and needs strong public pressure to have its common sense solutions translated into legislation.

Poisons in your Food   William Longood   *Pyramid Books*
>   A primer for housewives as a guide to the number of legally adulterated foods she is feeding her family.

Humus and the Farmer   Friend Sykes   *Faber and Faber*

This Farming Business	Friend Sykes	*Faber and Faber*
Plowman's Folly	E. Faulkner	*Grossett and Dunlap*
A Second Look	E. Faulkner	*University of Oklahoma Press*

A quartet of titles that will be of special interest to established farmers as they encompass the wide range of agricultural interests — both professional and personal.

Farmers of Forty Centuries F.H. King *Rodale Press*

A discussion of ancient eastern methods of agriculture that have kept the same fields fertile and healthy throughout the centuries.

How to have a Green Thumb Without an Aching Back Ruth Stout *Exposition Press*

How to use mulch rather than muscle and produce nutritious crops the natural, organic way.

Our Plundered Planet Fairfield Osborne *Pyramid Books*

Another early warning of the deterioration of our ecological heritage.

Harnessing the Earthworm T.J. Barrett *Bruce Humphries*

A fascinating study of that indispensable garden ally, the lowly earthworm.

Hunza John Tobe *McLeod*

A documentary on what is probably the healthiest group of people in the world and what makes them logical claimants to that title.

Gardening Without Poisons Beatrice Trum Hunter *Houghton-Miffin*
The Organic Way to Plant Protection J.I. Rodale, ed. *Rodale Press*

Of especial interest to the newly converted organic gardener to whom they will offer further arguments and solutions within the framework of organic farming.

Trees and Toadstools Dr. M.C. Rayner *Faber and Faber*

A study of the mycorrhizal association. The role of the fungi in the growth of conifers is of paramount importance to those interested in forestry.

Health and Nutrition   Sir Robert B. McCarrison   *Faber and Faber*
This is one of the few documented scientific works relating the
soil to the health of the plant, to the health of the animal, and
inferentially to the health of the human consumer. This should
be read by medical and dental students, nurses, dietitians, food
technologists, mothers, in fact, by all.

Those interested in the latest scientific investigation of normal
and diseased plants can read with advantage the work of Barranger in
the Polytechnical Institute in Paris, France and that of C.N. White at
the University of Sydney, Australia.

Index

tall versus short, 59
thinning, 100
See also charts for specific information.
Pesticides, biological magnification of, 49
cut costs of weeding carrots, 49
disaster, 50
effect on cole crops, 48
insects immunity to, 48
percentage effective, 48
potential damage, 5, 49
questioned, 5
risk, 50
selectivity of herbicides, 49
Pests, in ancient times, 44
as nature's censors, 44
biological control, 51-2
control methods, 52
man realizes their cause, 44
natural control, 50
pinpointing pest problems, 45-6
See also specific insects by name.
Phosphoric acid (phosphates), 39
pH scale, 58
Planting: *See specific vegetables by name.*
Plant reproduction, annuals, 40
asexuals, 41
biennials, 40
buddings, 42
cuttings, 41-2
layering, 41
perenniel, 40
sexual, 40
variations, 41
Plants, control of moisture for, 35
energy link, 34
environmental requirements, 35
life cycle, 24, 30, 34
moisture carries nutrients, 34
nutritional deficiencies, 35
oxygen regeneration, 35
Plowing, 31-2
Plowmans Folly, 32
Pollution, from excrement, 31
fertilizers from, 15
obligation to prevent, 5
pesticides, 15
Polyculture, advantages of, 24
experiment, 85
soil regeneration, 37

Population in soil, 29
Potash, 39
Potatoes, 55
blight prevention, 74
compacted soil, 61
cutting seed, 60
depth of seed, 100
dryness at digging for storage, 74
famine of 1847, 45
flea beetle in, 61
harvesting, 95
hilling, 61, 91
new, 72
prey predator relationship, 5
size of seed, 60
sprout inhibition, 75
time of emergence, 61
Protein, 12, 20
carbohydrate ratio, 47
fat ratio, 17

Quack grass, 46
Quiet Crisis, 14

Radishes, 64, 69
Rust fly, in carrots, 93, 95-6
Raspberries, 55, 105
freezing, 77
picking, 71
planting, 103
Red Stele, 5, 103
Report of the President's Science Advisory Committee, 6
Reynolds, Joshua, 7
Root Maggot, 64
Roots, development in corn, 65
exudates, 36-7
mycorrhizal association, 38
rotation, 38
symbiosis, 37
Romano Beans, 63, 79
Rotation of crops, 37

Salad preparation, 81
Scab, on potato, 5, 95
Seeds, numbers per ounce, 100
commercial producers of, 55
Sears, Paul, 39
St. John de Crèvècoeur, 22
Seeding, in dry weather, 90